# WISCONSIN WILDLIFE VIEWING GUIDE

**Mary K. Judd**

FALCON™

Falcon Press® Publishing Co., Inc.,
Helena, Montana

*"There will always be [passenger] pigeons in books and in museums, but these are effigies and images, dead to all hardships and to all delights. They know no urge of the seasons; they feel no kiss of sun, no lash of wind and weather."*

Aldo Leopold
*A Sand County Almanac*

This book is dedicated to the memory of the passenger pigeon, a bird that once thrived in such numbers their kind were said to have blackened the Wisconsin skies as they took flight. Today, a stone monument stands along a trail in Wyalusing State Park...a silent memorial to Wisconsin's last passenger pigeon. Have we learned from past mistakes? Will we allow today's wildlife to become stone monuments our children must visit to remind them of what was? We can only share the awe of wildlife with future generations if it exists for them to experience. Take care. Tread softly.

Copyright © 1995 by Falcon Press Publishing Co., Inc.,
Helena and Billings, Montana.
Illustrations copyright © 1995 by Defenders of Wildlife, Washington, D.C.
Published in cooperation with Defenders of Wildlife.

Defenders of Wildlife and its design are registered marks of Defenders of Wildlife, Washington, D.C.

Design, typesetting, and other prepress work by Falcon Press, Helena, Montana.
Printed in Hong Kong

Cataloging-in-Publication Data
Judd, Mary K.
   Wisconsin wildlife viewing guide / Mary K. Judd.
        p.    cm. -- (Watchable Wildlife Series)
   Includes index.
   ISBN 1-56044-208-5
   1. Wildlife viewing sites--Wisconsin--Guidebooks. 2. Wildlife watching--Wisconsin--Guidebooks. 3. Wisconsin--Guidebooks.
   I. Title. II. Series.
   QL214.J83   1994
   591.9775--dc20                               94-41259
                                                CIP

# ACKNOWLEDGMENTS

The author/state project manager and co-state project manager wish to give special thanks for advisory assistance to all Wisconsin Wildlife Viewing Guide Project Steering Committee members: Susan Nelson, Mary Newhouse, and Tony Rinaldi, USDA Forest Service; Ron Spry, U.S. Fish and Wildlife Service; Tom Gilbert, National Park Service; Karen Etter Hale, Wisconsin Audubon Council; and Ruel Fleming, Wisconsin Conservation Congress. Also, thanks for technical advice to: Randy Hoffman, Wisconsin Department of Natural Resources; Linda Parker, Steve Hoecker, USDA Forest Service; Winfield MacDonald, Wisconsin Division of Tourism; and Peter F. Rusch, Wisconsin Department of Transportation (WDOT). Also, we send our appreciation to all the on-site managers and others who provided nominations, interviews, tours, and text reviews.

The author/state project manager wishes to thank Carroll "Buzz" Besadny and Jim Addis for their support and encouragement, to Steve Miller whose foresight and sensitivity pioneered Wisconsin's venture into the world of Watchable Wildlife, to Tom Hauge, who guided Wisconsin DNR's involvement in this project, and to Chuck Spang (WDOT), who played a vital role assisting in the coordination of the project's signage. Special thanks also goes to Margaret Gaffney, Karen Etter Hale, and Ken Wood for their thoroughness in proofreading.

The co-state project manager offers thanks to Al Boss and Jim Cole, USDA Forest Service for their guidance and support and a special thanks to Cy Lyle, Wisconsin Audubon Council, for initiating and sustaining project partnership efforts.

**Author and State Project Manager:** Mary K. Judd, Ph.D.

**Co-state Project Manager:** Muriel Poindexter

**Project Assistant:** Janet L. Rolfsmeyer

**National Wildlife Viewing Guide**
**Program Manager:** Kate Davies,
Defenders of Wildlife

**Color illustrator:** Kandis Elliot

**Line illustrator:** Marian Fermani

**Front cover photo:** Common Loon, GREGORY K. SCOTT
**Back cover photos:** Lake Superior Shore, Big Bay State Park, KEVIN MAGEE;
Gray Wolf, MARK S. WERNER

# CONTENTS

# PROJECT SPONSORS

 DEFENDERS OF WILDLIFE is a national, nonprofit organization of more than 100,000 members and supporters dedicated to preserving the natural abundance and diversity of wildlife and its habitat. A 1-year membership is $20 and includes subscriptions to *Defenders*, an award-winning conservation magazine, and *Wildlife Adovocate*, an activist-oriented newsletter. To join, or for further information, write or call Defenders of Wildlife, 1101 14th Street NW, Suite 1400, Washington, DC 20005, (202) 682-9400.

 WISCONSIN DEPARTMENT OF NATURAL RESOURCES is charged with the responsibility of managing the state's wildlife, land, water, and air resources in trust for all citizens. Its many public properties, from wildlife areas, state parks and forests to natural areas, trails, and fisheries areas, provide excellent places to view wild animals in natural surroundings. For more information about Department properties with watchable wildlife opportunities, or to donate to the Watchable Wildlife Gift Account, contact Wisconsin DNR, 101 S. Webster, Box 7921, Madison. WI 53707-7921, (608) 266-2621.

 U.S.D.A. FOREST SERVICE is responsible for management of National Forest lands and their resources. As stewards of these lands, the Forest Service protects, restores, and manages them to provide various values to best serve tyhe needs of the American people. The Nicolet and Chequamegon national forests in northern Wisconsin are sponsers of this program to promote awareness and enjoyment of fish and wildlife on public lands. Contact the Chequamegon National Forest, 1170 4th Avenue South, Park Falls, WI 54552, (715) 762-2461 and the Nicolet National Forest, 68 S. Stevens St., Rhinelander, WI 54501, (715) 362-1300.

 DEPARTMENT OF DEFENSE (DOD) is the steward of about 25 million acres of land in the United States, many of which possess irreplaceable natural and cultural resources. The DOD is pleased to support the Watchable Wildlife Program through its Legacy Resource Management Program, a special initiative to enhance the conservation and restoration of natural and cultural resources on military land. For more information contact the Office of the Deputy Assistant Secretary of Defense (Environment), 400 Navy Drive, Suite 206, Arlington, VA 22202-2884.

 U.S. FISH AND WILDLIFE SERVICE is pleased to support this project in furtherance of its mission to conserve, protect, and enhance fish and wildlife resources and their habitats. In Wisconsin, the Service manages the Horicon, Necedah, Trempealeau, and Upper Mississippi River national wildlife refuges, the St. Croix and Leopold wetland management districts, and is active in wetland protection and restoration, and enforcement of federal fish and wildlife laws. U.S. Fish and Wildlife Service, W 4279 Headquarters Road, Mayville, WI 53050, (414) 387-2658.

 GE FUND is a trust which is authorized to make grants in the United States, and the GE FUND INC. is a corporation authorized to make grants in the United States and Internationally. They are the General Electric Company's vehicles for philanthropy in the areas of higher education, public policy, arts and culture, United Way, and the Matching Gifts Programs. Through the "More Gifts...More Givers" program, GE employees, retirees, and the Fund support the Wisconsin Trumpeter Swan Restoration Program, Wildlife Habitat Enhancement Council, The Watchable Wildlife Program, and other environmental stewardship projects. The GE FUND is located in Fairfield, CT.

WASTE MANAGEMENT OF WISCONSIN is part of WMX Technologies, Inc.., the world's largest environmental services company. We provide environmentally sound waste handling services through the reduction, recycling, treatment, and disposal of residential, commercial, and industrial wastes. Wisconsin's natural beauty is treasured by our employees, who wish you many happy hours as you explore and enjoy Wisconsin's spectacular scenic resources.

THE NATIONAL FISH AND WILDLIFE FOUNDATION is chartered by Congress to stimulate private giving to conservation and is an independent not-for-profit organization. It helped stimulate Partnerships for Wildlife challenge grants, which forged partnerships between public and private sectors to produce this guide and similar projects conserving the nation's fish, wildlife, and plants. National Fish and Wildlife Foundation, Bender Building, 1120 Connecticut Avenue NW Suite 900, Washington, DC 20036, (202) 857-0166.

The WISCONSIN DEPARTMENT OF TRANSPORTATION is responsible for providing safe, reliable, and well maintained highways throughout Wisconsin. Providing access to the state's recreational and scenic areas, and preserving the environment are among the department's highest priorities. The department also publishes the official highway map, which is available free-of-charge at welcome centers and visitor information offices across the state. Wisconsin Department of Transportation, 3617 Pierstorff Street, Madison, WI, 53704, (608) 246-3265.

KAYTEE PRODUCTS INCORPORATED. With a corporate philosophy committed to continuing and appreciating our privileged interaction with birds, Kaytee pursues its mission: to provide the highest quality foods and services for people's enjoyment of birds and small animals. At the Kaytee Avian Research Center, the opportunities for the advancement of avian stewardship in the form of nutritional studies, management investigations, conservation, and breeding biology are innumerable. With over 4,000 birds representing 100 species, the Kaytee Avian

Research Center is the largest exotic bird nutritional research center in the world, consisting of two major research facilities and an educational center. Cooperative projects are underway with universities, government agencies, research and conservation organizations such as the Cornell Laboratory of Ornithology, the Wild Bird Feeding Institute, U.S. Fish and Wildlife Service, and others. Projects such as these will ensure people's continued enjoyment of birds, not only today, but for tomorrow and for generations to come. Kaytee Products, Inc., P.O. Box 230, 521 Clay St., Chilton, WI 53014, (414) 849-2321.

ABC OUTDOOR ADVERTISING, INC., Pewaukee, Wisconsin, has been locally owned and operated since 1949, providing valuable service to local and national advertisers. ABC takes pride in its public service contributions, which exceeded $140,000 in production charges and advertising space during 1994. ABC is one of the first outdoor advertising firms to introduce landscaping around its structures to enhance the appearance of the area surrounding its signs. Efforts to preserve and improve the environment and make southeastern Wisconsin a better place to live are among ABC's highest priorities. We are pleased that we have been given the opportunity to help promote the Wisconsin Wildlife Viewing Guide. ABC Outdoor Advertising, Inc., 24600 Silvernail Road, Pewaukee, WI, 53012, (414) 542-8833.

Other important cooperators include: Wisconsin Society for Ornithology, National Park Service, Wisconsin Audubon Council, Wisconsin Audubon Council, Wisconsin Conservation Congress, and Madison Audubon Society.

Welcome to Wisconsin!

It is a pleasure to invite residents and visitors alike to explore Wisconsin's great outdoors. This book is your guide to some of the state's most inspiring natural treasures—its wildlife.

Each season offers its own unique wildlife viewing opportunities. Across Wisconsin witness the springtime return of thousands of migratory birds—from tiny yellow warblers to giant Canada geese. In summer watch families of river otter play along the banks of the Chippewa Flowage. Fall brings the spectacle of several thousand sandhill cranes gathering at Sandhill Wildlife Area, and in winter, majestic bald eagles fish the icy waters of the Lower Wisconsin State Riverway.

Finding, observing, and enjoying the state's wildlife has now been made easier, thanks to the *Wisconsin Wildlife Viewing Guide*. Developed cooperatively by more than a dozen agencies and conservation groups, it encompasses federal, state, county, and private viewing areas throughout the state.

Regardless of where you live or travel in Wisconsin there are sites in this guide near you. Watch the highways for the brown road signs with the white binocular symbol. They lead to each of the sites described in the guide and to memorable opportunities to enjoy Wisconsin's rich wildlife heritage.

Sincerely,

Tommy G. Thompson
Governor

# INTRODUCTION

Wisconsin is a place of natural beauty. From northern boreal forests to sand barrens, from Lake Michigan shorelines to backwaters of the St. Croix River, from prairies to oak forests, and from pine groves to cedar swamps, this diverse landscape supports an equally diverse array of wildlife. This includes 657 species of mammals, birds, reptiles, amphibians, and fish, and several thousand types of insects and other invertebrates.

Throughout the state look for white-tailed deer. The northern highlands are home to coyote, beaver, porcupine, and sharp-tailed grouse. Numerous freshwater lakes host breeding populations of bald eagle, osprey, and loon. One can experience the fall flight of several hundred thousand Canada geese descending on Horicon Marsh, while the Mississippi River serves as a major flyway for waterfowl, notably tundra swans and canvasback ducks. You may get a rare glimpse of some of Wisconsin's endangered species such as the gray wolf, trumpeter swan, peregrine falcon, and Karner blue butterfly. A springtime trip to one of the state's many wetlands will be met with a chorus of frogs and toads. The seasonal runs of trout and salmon and the springtime spawning of lake sturgeon provide spectacles not to be missed.

The viewing sites featured in this guide reflect the wide variety of habitats and wildlife that abound here. Nearly two hundred potential viewing sites were considered, and stringent standards were used to evaluate and choose seventy-six of them. Many worthy sites were not included due to space limitations, and several more were eliminated to protect wildlife and habitat from damage. All areas offer unique or exceptional opportunities to view native free-roaming wildlife.

This guide was designed for both the casual observer and serious wildlife watcher, offering a spectrum of viewing experiences ranging from remote backwoods trails to urban preserves. Many sites have nature centers with brochures and other interpretive materials to make your excursions more interesting and rewarding.

To view wildlife in a natural setting—a sunset flight of sandhill cranes, a red fox with her pups—is to feel awe, excitement, wonder. These experiences become the foundation upon which each of us builds an appreciation for and an understanding of the natural systems and diversity of wildlife that surround us.

So, whether you're off to watch the drama of prairie chickens on their booming grounds or heading out to marvel at the vast flocks of tundra swans, may these experiences inspire you to support agencies and private organizations that are working to safeguard Wisconsin's wildlife legacy.

# THE NATIONAL WATCHABLE WILDLIFE PROGRAM

In 1986, the President's Commission on America's Great Outdoors identified wildlife viewing as one of the nation's most popular outdoor activities. Public interest in wildlife continues to grow rapidly at both the national and state levels. A recent survey conducted by the U.S. Fish and Wildlife Service showed that more than 85 percent of Wisconsin residents regularly participate in watchable wildlife activities. As public demand grows and as wildlife habitat is altered or lost to development, the cost of providing such recreational opportunities is escalating.

For many years, public fish and wildlife areas, refuges, preserves, and habitat management programs—which benefit non-game wildlife as well as game animals—have been funded almost exclusively by hunters and anglers through license fees and taxes on fishing and hunting equipment. Though hunting in Wisconsin remains a strong tradition, national trends indicate that participation in this outdoor sport is on the decline. This has generated concern about the future source of wildlife conservation and recreation dollars.

The *Wisconsin Wildlife Viewing Guide* is part of a national response to the increased interest in wildlife viewing and the need to develop new support and funding for wildlife programs. As part of the National Watchable Wildlife Program, coordinated by Defenders of Wildlife, federal and state agencies in Wisconsin have formed a partnership with conservation and other organizations to promote wildlife viewing, conservation, and education. The *Wisconsin Wildlife Viewing Guide* is an important first step in the effort. The sites described in this guide are part of a national wildlife viewing network. Sites across the country will be marked with the brown and white binocular sign appearing on the cover of this book. Look for these signs in your travels.

Though not every site described in this book is fully developed yet, site enhancement is the next step. As time goes on, wildlife watchers will find new facilities such as interpretive signs, trails, viewing blinds or platforms, and provisions for parking and restrooms. Ultimately, the goal of the Watchable Wildlife Program is to create an appreciation for the natural world in all its diversity and an understanding that all plants and animals play an important and unique role in the health of the world's ecosystems.

Use this guide to plan outings that coincide with peak wildlife viewing periods. Consult it while traveling for interesting side trips and take advantage of on-site education programs. Become an active partner in resource stewardship by supporting wildlife agency and private efforts to fund wildlife programs. We must work together to assure that our wildlife heritage survives and prospers for the health and quality of our natural environment and for the enjoyment of ourselves and future generations.

# WISCONSIN'S BIODIVERSITY: MAKING THE CONNECTION

Wisconsin is a place of connections...a place where boreal forests of the north meet hardwood forests of the east and grasslands of the west. These ecological crossroads create a state with great biological diversity, or *biodiversity*. Very simply, biodiversity refers to the variety of plants and animals and the natural processes that maintain healthy natural communities.

Prior to European settlement, the rich, diverse quality of Wisconsin's natural communities was intact. Subsequent years of logging, farming, and urban development have posed significant problems. Along with environmental pollution, ecosystems have become less complex and habitats have been fragmented. Some species couldn't survive these impacts and disappeared from the state. So went the bison and whooping crane. Animals such as the trumpeter swan, wolf, and some interior forest songbirds are still struggling to maintain a foothold. Others, like deer and cowbirds, have flourished because they readily adapted to these altered habitats. People have also affected native ecosystems by introducing exotic species. Buckthorn, tatarian honeysuckle, garlic mustard, and purple loosestrife, along with starling, house sparrow, rusty crayfish, and zebra mussel, have literally taken over some parts of the Wisconsin landscape, posing severe threats to native species.

The challenge for us in the future is to continue to explore new ways for our growing human population to live more compatibly with our natural environment. People are as much a component of the ecosystem as are the plants and animals. Although the basic elements of Wisconsin's natural heritage remain intact, cooperative efforts must be maintained to preserve its rich biodiversity.

*Horicon Marsh, once nearly destroyed by dredging, draining, plowing, and overharvesting, has been restored to become Wisconsin's most popular wildlife viewing area. This wetland of international importance is a symbol of Wisconsin's rich and diverse natural heritage.* KEVIN MAGEE

# VIEWING TIPS

Seeing a wild animal in its natural habitat is a rewarding experience. Much of the excitement of wildlife viewing stems from the fact that you can never be sure what you will see. Here are a number of things that you can do in preparation for a trip to greatly increase your odds of seeing wildlife.

**Visit when animals are active.** Generally there is more wildlife activity in the first and last hours of daylight. However, some animals are active at night.

**Wildlife viewing is often seasonal.** Wildlife activity peaks in Wisconsin during April and May when large numbers of migratory birds return to the state and animals are busy raising their young. Activity pulses again in September and October as migratory birds prepare for flights south and mammals make arrangements for the long winter months. Consult a field guide for additional information, or call the site owner for an update before you visit.

**Learn to be still, silent, and patient.** Quick movements will scare wildlife. Take a few steps, then stop, look, and listen. Use your ears to locate birds or the movements of other animals. Walk into the wind if possible, avoiding brittle sticks and leaves. Use trees and vegetation as a blind. Your parked car, or a canoe, make good viewing blinds.

**Learn about the animals and their "calling cards."** Though Wisconsin's wildlife is very abundant, you may, at times, miss an opportunity to observe them. Learn to listen for animal sounds and be alert for signs, such as tracks in mud or snow, nibbled branches, gnawed nuts, or runways and tunnels, to give you clues about the presence of wildlife. Use field guides and other resources, and learn what the animal looks like, where it lives, and its habits.

**Come prepared.** Expect insects, especially during warm summer months. Bring along repellents and protective clothing, and tuck pant legs into socks. Plan ahead for viewing trips, and bring all of the things you, your group, or your vehicle may require. Review the site account in this guide before you visit, checking for warnings about road conditions and weather.

Look for additional wildlife viewing hints throughout the pages of this guide.

## VIEWING ETHICS AND RESPONSIBILITIES

Most wildlife viewers care a great deal about wildlife and wildlife habitat. However, even those with sincere concern can unknowingly place wildlife or themselves at great risk. Observing the following tips will ensure a safe experience for you, for others, and for the animals being watched.

**Don't disturb the animals.** Please avoid touching wildlife or moving too close to the animals, their nests, or dens. Disturbances may result in an animal abandoning its young, injuring itself as it tries to escape, or displaying aggressive behavior.

**Never chase or harass animals.** This may result in an animal spending valuable energy needed to survive. Viewing trips will be more successful if pets are left at home.

**Don't feed the wildlife.** Some animals that become accustomed to handouts may lose their natural fear of humans and may approach cars, increasing their risk of traffic mortality. Also, waterfowl may delay their winter migration, causing higher risk of death.

**Don't pick up orphaned or sick animals.** Wild animals rarely abandon their young. Usually the parents are hidden nearby, waiting for visitors to leave before they return. If you suspect an animal is sick or injured, leave it alone, and report its location to the site manager.

**Leave the site undisturbed.** Respect rules regarding pets, collecting, restricted areas, viewing hours, etc. Stay on marked trails and be careful not to trample plant life. Pick up litter and dispose of it properly.

**Respect the rights of other recreationists at a site.** Be considerate when approaching wildlife that is already being viewed by others. Moving too quickly or loudly may spoil the experience for everyone.

**Honor the rights of private landowners** at or near viewing sites. Always gain permission before entering their property.


## HOW TO USE THIS GUIDE

This guide is divided into six travel regions, each tab coded for quick reference. Wildlife viewing sites are listed and located on a map at the beginning of each region. Each site includes the following elements to help describe and interpret wildlife and habitats you may see.

**Description:** This gives a brief account of the habitat and wildlife.

**Viewing Information:** This section expands on the site description and gives the seasonal likelihood of spotting wildlife at the site. It may include information about access, parking, and *WARNINGS* in capital letters.

**Directions:** Written directions are provided for most sites. If the site is slightly difficult to locate, a full-color map is provided. Roads, nearby towns, access points, and other viewing information are printed on these maps. *NOTE: PLEASE SUPPLEMENT THE MAPS IN THIS GUIDE WITH AN UP-TO-DATE WISCONSIN ROAD MAP,* such as the *Wisconsin Atlas and Gazetter.*

**Ownership:** Provides the name of the agency, organization, or company that owns or manages the site. The telephone number listed may be used to obtain more information.

**Recreation and Facility Symbols:** These indicate some of the facilities and opportunities available at each site. The managing agency can provide more information. The camping, restaurant, lodging, and boat ramp symbols mean that these facilities are available within the site boundaries.

## WILDLIFE ICONS

Songbirds
Perching Birds

Wading
Birds

Upland
Birds

Waterfowl

Birds of
Prey

Shorebirds

Fish

Reptiles,
Amphibians

Hoofed
Mammals

Freshwater
Mammals

Carnivores

Small
Mammals

Bats

Insects

Wildflowers

## FACILITIES AND RECREATION ICONS

Parking

Entry Fee

Restrooms

Trails

Barrier-Free

Boat Ramp

Small Boats

Large Boats

Picnic

Restaurant

Lodging

Cross-Country
Skiing

Camping

Hunting

Bicycling

In this guide the barrier-free symbol means there is at least car viewing and one barrier-free restroom on site. Accessible trails or structures are often noted. Many other sites are accessible to varying degrees.

The hunting symbol will be found only at sites at which hunting is a primary use for the property. Please call the site managers for specific dates and more information.

## SITE OWNER/MANAGER ABBREVIATIONS

| | |
|---|---|
| ACE | U.S. Army Corps of Engineers |
| NPS | National Park Service |
| PVT | Private land |
| TNC | The Nature Conservancy |
| USFS | USDA Forest Service |
| USFWS | U.S. Fish & Wildlife Service |
| WDNR | Wisconsin Department of Natural Resources |
| WDOT | Wisconsin Department of Transportation |

# WISCONSIN
*Wildlife Viewing Areas*

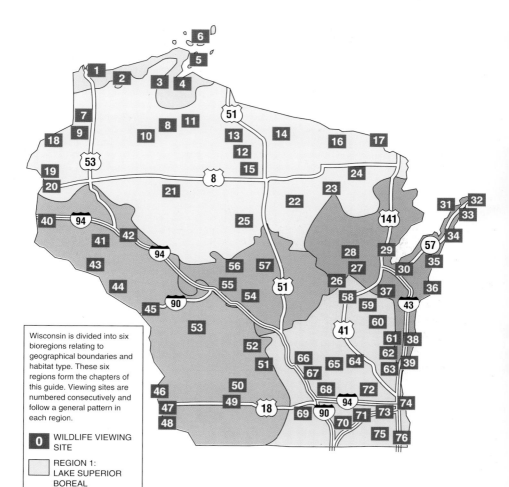

Wisconsin is divided into six bioregions relating to geographical boundaries and habitat type. These six regions form the chapters of this guide. Viewing sites are numbered consecutively and follow a general pattern in each region.

**0**    WILDLIFE VIEWING SITE

REGION 1: LAKE SUPERIOR BOREAL

REGION 2: NORTHERN HIGHLANDS

REGION 3: LAKE MICHIGAN LOWLAND

REGION 4: WESTERN DRIFTLESS UPLAND

REGION 5: CENTRAL SANDS TRANSITION

REGION 6: SOUTHEASTERN MORAINES

## HIGHWAY SIGNS

As you travel in Wisconsin and other states, look for these signs on highways and other roads. They identify the route to follow to reach wildlife viewing sites.

15

# REGION ONE: LAKE SUPERIOR BOREAL

A bit of Canada may be found along Wisconsin's northern border, where majestic, snow-covered evergreen spires create scenes of grandeur. Moist, forceful winds blow inland from Lake Superior, producing cold winters and springs, cool summers, yet relatively mild autumn weather. The gently rolling hills of this region are cloaked in hemlock, sugar maple, paper birch, white spruce, and pine, with swales dominated by balsam fir, white cedar, tamarack, and black spruce. The area's sphagnum bogs are rich in peat.

Typical wildlife of this region includes the spruce grouse, black-backed woodpecker, red squirrel, pine marten, fisher, snowshoe hare, porcupine, and raven. Great gray owls winter in these forests, while snowy owls hunt the grasslands and lakeshore. The evening grosbeak, white-winged crossbill, red-breasted nuthatch, boreal chickadee, and northern parula warbler are among the songbirds found here.

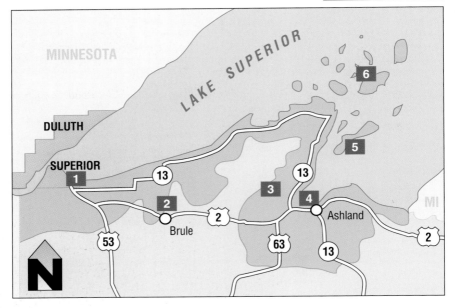

WILDLIFE VIEWING SITES
1   Wisconsin Point
2   Brule River State Forest
3   Chequamegon National Forest: Moquah Pine Barrens
4   Fish Creek Slough
5   Big Bay State Park
6   Apostle Islands National Lakeshore

# 1. WISCONSIN POINT

**Description:** A peninsula on Lake Superior, Wisconsin Point has many diverse habitats. One of the state's premier birding areas, it acts as a rest stop for songbirds, raptors, and shorebirds traveling around the lake during migration.

**Viewing Information:** Birding is most impressive here in March. Look for bald eagle, and great black-backed and glaucous gull. Waterfowl and raptors arrive in April. Scan the lake in May for red-necked and pied-billed grebes, loons, and other waterbirds. Peak warbler migration occurs around May 15 when thousands of migrants, such as mourning and northern parula warblers, stop here. Shorebirds such as ruddy turnstone and buff-breasted sandpiper appear as summer arrives. Check the bay's mudflats throughout summer for northern harrier and merlin. Watch for sharp-shinned and broad-winged hawk, and many warbler species among fall migrants. On cold winter days, search for snowy owl on the lake ice and in open field areas, and red crossbill and pine grosbeak in mature pines.

*Directions: From Superior take US 2/53 east to Moccasin Mike Road. Take the first left (Wisconsin Point Road) to the end.*

**Ownership:** City of Superior (715) 394-0200

**Size:** 3-mile stretch of land     **Closest Town:** Superior

*Snowy owls visit northern Wisconsin each winter. Watch for them perched on fenceposts, road signs, or even urban neon signs.*
GREGORY K. SCOTT

## 2. BRULE RIVER STATE FOREST

**Description:** An exceptional trout stream, boreal (northern) forest, and black spruce/white cedar/balsam fir bogs characterize this paradise for northwoods birds and mammals.

**Viewing Information:** Boreal forests and northern hardwoods provide nesting habitat for ovenbird, vireos, thrushes, and a variety of woodpeckers. Boreal- and bog-nesting warblers are found in northern conifers. Eagle and osprey search the expanse of river for trout and non-native salmon, while wood turtle trek along sandy shores. Beaver, muskrat, and river otter are present year-round. Black bear present from spring through early fall. Walk Lake Superior's shoreline in search of shorebirds in spring and fall. Winter is a special time for wildlife watching on the Bois Brule River. At dusk, ravens engage in ritualized aerial displays and calls before heading off to roost. The elusive bobcat, which preys on abundant snowshoe hare, leaves tracks in the snow. On rare occasions, northern hawk owl may visit. Great gray and snowy owl hunt for meadow voles and deer mice. Black-backed woodpecker and boreal chickadee are typical. Self-guided nature trail and barrier-free boat landing.

**Directions:** *Take US 2 south in Brule and turn south on Ranger Station Road to DNR Headquarters.*

**Ownership:** WDNR (715) 372-4866
**Size:** 47,000 acres    **Closest Town:** Brule

*The bobcat's speed, stealth, and camouflaged coat make it an elusive predator, difficult for wildlife watchers to glimpse.* DENVER BRYAN

## 3. CHEQUAMEGON NATIONAL FOREST: MOQUAH PINE BARRENS

**Description:** An anomaly in the boreal forest, these pine barrens are sandy scrublands with stands of jack pine and aspen which support a diverse community of wildlife.

**Viewing Information:** Coyote, white-tailed deer, woodchuck, and grassland sparrows are present in this open habitat. Managers use timber harvesting and prescribed burning to keep this area from reverting to forest so that badger, plains pocket gopher, eastern bluebird, tree swallow, red-tailed hawk, and upland sandpiper may continue to survive. Gray wolves and black bear occasionally use the area. Wildlife viewing by vehicle. Wildflowers are on display spring through summer. *SITE IS REMOTE; MAP IS RECOMMENDED FOR EXPLORING ADJACENT GRAVEL ROADS.* Contact Washburn Office for road conditions and map.

**Directions:** *From Ashland take US 2 west 12 miles. Turn right on Forest Road 236. Go 6 miles to the barrens. Driving tour is signed.*

**Ownership:** USFS (715) 373-2667
**Size:** 9,336 acres
**Closest Town:** Washburn

## 4. FISH CREEK SLOUGH

**Description:** URBAN SITE. Fish Creek's cattail sloughs and Chequamegon Bay provide excellent habitat for a large variety and high concentration of waterfowl and shorebirds.

**Viewing Information:** A scenic overlook in Ashland's Prentice Park provides a good view of the sloughs and Lake Superior. In March and April, look for ducks and tundra swan along the lower trails which lead to an observation platform. Diving ducks and horned grebe feed in the open bay waters, while mallards, teals, herons, and ring-billed gull congregate along the marsh edges. Shorebirds, such as the Hudsonian godwit and red-necked phalarope, arrive along the sand flats as waterfowl depart. Sora, yellow-headed blackbird, least bittern, black tern, and marsh wrens may be found in the cattails during a summer canoe outing. Bald eagle and osprey occur regularly and snowy owl make occasional visits in winter.

**Directions:** *In Ashland take US 2 west to Prentice Park where access is obtained on the south side.*

**Ownership:** City of Ashland (715)682-7071; WDNR (715) 372-4866
**Size:** 700 acres
**Closest Town:** Ashland

## 5. BIG BAY STATE PARK

**Description:** Located on Madeline Island, the largest of 22 Apostle Islands, this park sports rugged wooded cliffs with dramatic views of Lake Superior.

**Viewing Information:** Explore wildlife from an interpretive boardwalk that traverses a fragile bog, barrier beach, and lagoon where palm warbler, common loon, merlin, and painted turtle are present beginning in May. Broad-winged hawks circle above. Search for ruby-crowned kinglet, bay-breasted warbler, and pileated woodpecker in old-growth hemlocks and Bonaparte's gull, sanderling, and dunlin along the beach. Look for common merganser and lesser scaup on Lake Superior. In late summer the shoreline ladybug migration is a special treat. Island mammals include deer, coyote, bear, and beaver. Ferry runs approximately April 1 to January 1.

*Directions: Take ferry from Bayfield to LaPointe. Follow signs to park, 7 miles from LaPointe.*

**Ownership:** WDNR  (715) 779-3346; Madeline Island (715) 747-6425
**Size:** 2,350 acres    **Closest Town:** La Pointe

*Scenic Lake Superior islands provide diverse habitats for wildlife. Isolation from the populated mainland provides wildlife with refuge from extensive development and human intrusion.* KEVIN MAGEE

## 6 . APOSTLE ISLANDS NATIONAL LAKESHORE

**Description:** Scattered over 750 square miles of Lake Superior waters, the 22 Apostle Islands support a northwoods wildlife community associated with hemlock hardwood and boreal forests.

**Viewing Information:** More than 200 species of birds may be found on the islands during spring and fall migration, Outer and Long islands in particular. Large numbers of broad-winged hawks migrate through each spring. Bald eagles are one of more than 100 species that breed here. Stockton, Sand, and Raspberry islands offer good opportunities to watch a variety of warblers and thrushes in the breeding season of May and June. Long Island is great for spotting waterfowl and shorebirds. Spring peeper, wood frog, and eastern garter snake are common on many islands. Though black bear are seldom seen, they are abundant on Stockton and Sand islands. In late September and October, large numbers of peregrine falcons and merlins use Outer Island as staging grounds during migration. Barrier-free visitor center, ranger programs, and trails enhance the visit. Excursion boats run approximately Memorial Day through the first week in October.

*Directions: Take WI 13 north to Bayfield. Follow signs to National Park Service visitor center.*

**Ownership:** NPS (715) 779-3397
**Size:** 21 islands and 12-mile strip of mainland to equal 42,140 acres
**Closest Town:** Bayfield

## BINOC BASICS: ESSENTIAL TOOLS FOR THE WILDLIFE WATCHER

Binoculars come in sizes such as 7x35, 8x40, and 10x50. The smaller number refers to how large the animal will be magnified compared to the unaided eye. A "7x" means that the animal is magnified 7 times. A downside of larger magnifications is that your hand movements will be magnified that much more. A bird in a tree will be harder to find with a 10x magnification than with a 7x because even your breathing will cause the image to move. The larger number in the couplet refers to the diameter of the larger lens that faces the animal. The larger that number, the more light will be gathered, hence the better for viewing wildlife in dim light.

# REGION TWO: NORTHERN HIGHLANDS

Dotted with thousands of freshwater lakes, this northern region supports sugar maple, hemlock, and yellow birch, along with white and red pine. Peat bogs are prevalent and dominated by black spruce, tamarack, and white cedar. Though much of this country is enveloped in a cool, leafy canopy, other areas support open, savanna-like pine barrens and sand prairies.

These are the forests of the ruffed grouse and goshawk, of the fisher and its snowshoe hare prey, as well as the black bear and barred owl. Remote areas support small packs of gray wolves. White-tailed deer move to cedar groves in heavy winters. Numerous lakes boast breeding populations of bald eagle, osprey, and common loon. The barrens are home to badger, sharp-tailed grouse, pocket gopher, and eastern bluebird.

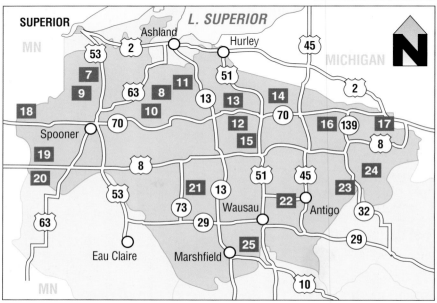

## WILDLIFE VIEWING SITES

7   Gordon Dam Park
8   Chequamegon National Forest: Lynch Creek Impoundment
9   Namekagon Barrens Wildlife Area
10   Chippewa Flowage
11   Chequamegon National Forest: Day Lake
12   Chequamegon National Forest: Popple Creek/Wilson Flowage
13   Turtle-Flambeau Flowage
14   Northern Highland-American Legion State Forest
15   Willow Flowage
16   Nicolet National Forest: Anvil Trails
17   Nicolet National Forest: Brule River
18   Crex Meadows Wildlife Area
19   Saint Croix National Scenic Riverway
20   Interstate Park
21   Chequamegon National Forest: Chequamegon Waters Flowage
22   Marathon County Forest: Bitzke Birdwalk
23   Nicolet National Forest: Cathedral Pines
24   Nicolet National Forest: Knowles Creek Impoundment
25   George W. Mead Wildlife Area

## 7. GORDON DAM PARK

**Description:** Gordon Dam marks the entrance to the pristine St. Croix National Scenic Riverway. Its flowage and marshes provide excellent viewing of aquatic and terrestrial northwoods wildlife.

**Viewing Information:** The lookout point on County Hwy. Y, with good barrier-free access, allows an aerial view of the flowage. Along the dike path which crosses the park's dam, look for white-tailed deer, bear, and bobcat. Snowshoe hare, coyote, and red fox are common. The patient observer may hear a wolf howl. From a quiet canoe, watch as bald eagle, mink, muskrat, otter, and beaver work the open waters. Spring through fall, ring-necked and black duck, blue-winged teal, and Canada goose inhabit the flowage along with American bittern. An auto tour of northern habitats is available at the Solon Springs office. *COUNTY HWY. Y MAY BE IMPASSABLE IN WINTER.*

**Directions:** *From Gordon travel west 7 miles on County Hwy. Y. The park and dam are at end of highway.*

**Ownership:** Douglas County (715) 378-2219
**Size:** 80 acres    **Closest Town:** Gordon

## 8. CHEQUAMEGON NATIONAL FOREST: LYNCH CREEK IMPOUNDMENT

**Description:** In the heart of a pine and tamarack forest, Lynch Creek Impoundment is a wetland managed specifically for waterfowl.

**Viewing Information:** Ring-necked and wood duck and hooded merganser breed in this secluded habitat spring through summer. Beaver, mink, raccoon, red fox, coyote, and deer seek this site year-round for food and water. Bullfrog, spring peeper, and crayfish are food for river otter. The water level is drawn down every 3 to 5 years to enhance nutrient cycling, which encourages aquatic vegetation for wildlife. During warm months, eagle and osprey make occasional visits. The site features a barrier-free viewing platform, hard-packed surface trails, and wetland vistas. *REMOTE GRAVEL ROADS MAY BE IMPASSABLE IN WINTER.*

**Directions:** *From Hayward take WI 77 east 23 miles. Turn left (north) on Forest Road (FR) 203; proceed 6 miles. Turn left (west) on FR 622. Site is less than 0.5 mile on left.*

**Ownership:** USFS (715) 634-4821
**Size:** 30 acres    **Closest Town:** Cable

## 9. NAMEKAGON BARRENS WILDLIFE AREA

**Description:** One of only four public properties containing shrub prairie habitat reminiscent of the rare pine barrens ecosystem, this site is noted for the springtime dancing ritual of sharp-tailed grouse. Active logging and prescribed burning keep the forest from enclosing this open habitat.

**Viewing Information:** A great place for viewing grassland birds in the north, the barrens is home to upland sandpiper, eastern kingbird, eastern bluebird, tree swallow, and clay-colored and vesper sparrow throughout spring and summer. Search the brush for gray catbird, brown thrasher, yellow warbler, rufous-sided towhee, and Brewer's blackbird. The highlight is watching the

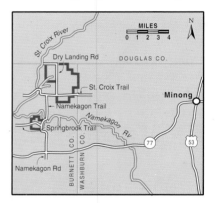

spectacular early spring drama of dawn-dancing sharp-tailed grouse. Viewing blinds are available; call for details. Prairie grasses and flowers provide a changing display from spring through late summer. June and July are particularly colorful. Shy badgers and abundant deer, along with an occasional black bear or gray wolf, claim this open habitat as home base. *REMOTE SITE WITH SAND AND GRAVEL ROADS; MAY BE IMPASSABLE IN WINTER. PLEASE REMAIN ON TRAILS.*

*Directions: See map.*

**Ownerships:** Burnett County; Management: WDNR (715) 635-4091
**Size:** 5,049 acres    **Closest Town:** Minong

Once four to five million acres of pine and oak barrens thrived in Wisconsin. The sandy soils of these habitats support a wide array of prairie plants and brush. The barrens existed because wildfires kept the encroaching pine and oak forests from invading. Today, these barrens need to be actively managed by clearcutting and prescribed burning to keep their vistas open and available for a diversity of wildlife, including sharp-tailed grouse, bluebird, bobcat, badger, and the endangered gray wolf and Karner blue butterfly.

## 10. CHIPPEWA FLOWAGE

**Description:** Northwoods wildlife abounds in and around this vast flowage—233 miles of rugged pine and aspen shoreline cut by numerous bays, channels, and floating bogs. The waters are dotted with hundreds of forested islands.

**Viewing Information:** Travel by boat or canoe to fully appreciate the abundant wildlife throughout the warm months. Look for the splash of otter, muskellunge, and northern pike. Bald eagles perch overhead, while common loons serenade. Osprey, great blue heron, kingfisher, puddle and diving ducks, beaver, and mink are common. Raccoon and deer venture near shore at dusk. Flashlights will help catch their eye shine. *CALL WDNR FOR SHINING LAWS.* Maps and boat rentals available on County Hwy. CC. *MAP RECOMMENDED. DO NOT APPROACH OR DISTURB LOONS.*

*Directions: From Hayward take County Hwy. B east. Turn right on County Hwy. CC, which cuts through middle of flowage. Stop at Herman's Landing for maps, information, and boat rentals.*

**Ownership:** WDNR (715) 634-6513; USFS (715) 634-4821; Lac Courte Oreilles (715) 865-2329

**Size:** 22,200 acres    **Closest Town:** Hayward

*The aptly-named sharp-tailed grouse provides an early spring wildlife watching spectacle not to be missed. Males conduct their courtship dance on open brush prairie habitats.*
SCOTT NIELSEN

25

## 11. CHEQUAMEGON NATIONAL FOREST: DAY LAKE

**Description:** A variety of habitats, including floating sphagnum-tamarack bogs, attract waterfowl, raptors, and northwoods mammals to this site.

**Viewing Information:** Barrier-free viewing platforms, 2 nesting structures, and shoreline hiking trails provide great opportunities to watch osprey and bald eagle. The shore attracts plovers and sandpipers during migration as well as pine marten, fisher, red squirrel, white-tailed deer, and black bear. Muskellunge occasionally jump in the water. Kingfisher, great blue heron, and loon also inhabit this site which is easily explored by canoe. To reach interpretive trail, cross dam and travel along shore.

*Directions: From Clam Lake take County Hwy. M west 0.33 mile. Go past County Hwy. GG. Follow signs for boat landing and day use area. Park near picnic area.*

**Ownership:** USFS (715) 264-2511
**Size:** 100 acres    **Closest Town:** Clam Lake

## 12. CHEQUAMEGON NATIONAL FOREST: POPPLE CREEK/WILSON FLOWAGE

**Description:** Popple Creek Trail leads wildlife watchers along a glacial ridge to an expansive vista of Wilson Flowage where waterfowl and wetland wildlife abound.

**Viewing Information:** In spring look for ring-necked and wood duck, blue-winged teal, hooded merganser, and yellow-headed blackbird which regularly nest along the wetland shores. In summer, osprey occupy the distant nesting platform on an island as bald eagles soar overhead and common loons serenade below. Migrating tundra swan, Canada and snow goose, common goldeneye, and bufflehead return each fall. Follow the trail past a beaver dam, and search for tracks of snowshoe hare, red fox, coyote, and the secretive fisher. Interpretive signs along the trail enhance the wildlife watching experience. Carry-in canoe access only. *REMOTE GRAVEL ROADS MAY BE IMPASSABLE IN WINTER AND AFTER HEAVY RAINS.*

*Directions: From Fifield go 13 miles east on WI 70. Turn right on Forest Road 137 (Riley Lake Road). Go 6 miles. Turn right on Gates Lake Road and go less than 0.5 mile to parking lot.*

**Ownership:** USFS (715) 762-2461
**Size:** 266 acres    **Closest Town:** Fifield

# 13. TURTLE-FLAMBEAU FLOWAGE

**Description:** An impressive artificial impoundment with more than 180 miles of white pine and birch shoreline and hundreds of small islands, this flowage is located near Mercer, Loon Capital of Wisconsin.

**Viewing Information:** This scenic flowage boasts the highest number of bald eagle, osprey, and common loon breeding pairs in the state. *LOONS ARE ESPE-CIALLY SENSITIVE TO HUMAN DISTURBANCE; PLEASE WATCH FROM A RESPECTFUL DISTANCE.* Osprey and eagle are busy each spring with court-ship rituals, followed by never-ending trips from nest to fishing ground as they feed their young. Hooded merganser, giant Canada goose, great blue heron, double-crested cormorant, black tern, and yellow-headed blackbird share the waters with these northwoods birds as do fisher, mink, muskrat, beaver, otter, and bobcat. The merlin, a rare falcon, nests here. Wolf, black bear, and moose are occasionally seen. White-tailed deer are common. Wildlife viewing is best from boat. Rentals available in Mercer and at resorts on flowage. Maps, information, and a Northwoods Auto Tour guide for car viewing are available from WDNR office in Mercer. *FLOWAGE MAPS HIGHLY RECOMMENDED. BOATERS USE CAUTION; MANY SUB-MERGED STUMPS AND ROCKS.*

**Directions:** *See map.*

**Ownership:** WDNR (715) 476-2646
**Size:** 14,000 acres
**Closest Town:** Mercer

*Common loons nest and raise their young on many northwoods lakes. Listen for their haunting yodel, but steer clear of their nests.* STEPHEN J. LANG

# 14. NORTHERN HIGHLAND-AMERICAN LEGION STATE FOREST

**Description:** Wisconsin's largest state property contains a diversity of northern timber types interspersed with grasslands, marshes, and more than 900 lakes. This site provides ideal habitats for northwoods wildlife, including one of the largest concentrations of nesting bald eagles in Wisconsin.

**Viewing Information:** The forest comes alive late April through May with spring wildflowers and migrant songbirds: ruby-throated hummingbird, white-throated sparrow, scarlet tanager, and whip-poor-will. In early June, look for colorful butterflies such as tiger swallowtails. In summer, search for sharp-shinned hawk, great horned owl, raven, and American bittern. White-tailed deer, snowshoe hare, black bear, fisher, otter, red fox, coyote, beaver, and mink are common, while pine marten, gray wolf, and spruce grouse are more elusive. Red-breasted nuthatch, yellow-bellied sapsucker, and pileated woodpecker nest here. In winter look for grosbeaks, goshawk, Canada jay, and snowy owl. The state forest is home to several endangered, threatened, or sensitive species, from the spotted salamander, wood turtle, and Cooper's hawk, to the bald eagle, osprey, and common loon. *PLEASE KEEP A RESPECTFUL DISTANCE FROM THESE BIRDS AND THEIR NESTS.* Excellent roads and trail systems allow viewing by car, bike, boat, canoe, or foot. From Star Lake Nature Trail, witness waves of warblers lured by the insect hatch in mid-May. Wander through stands of large hemlock, yellow birch, and white pine on Clear Lake Nature Trail, where barred owl and little brown bat seek shelter. Canoe the Manitowish River where waterfowl, and green and great blue heron find refuge in its marshes and sloughs. Bearskin State Trail, with multiple access points, traverses forests, bogs, and lakes featuring eagle, osprey, common loon, beaver, and muskrat. Woodruff Fish Hatchery offers summer tours. Check for summer naturalist programs.

*Directions: See map.*

**Ownership:** WDNR (715) 385-2727
**Size:** 223,000 acres
**Closest Town:** Boulder Junction

## 15. WILLOW FLOWAGE

**Description:** Experience the quiet seclusion of the northwoods among the aspen, white and red pine, birch, and maple that cloak the islands and more than 100 miles of scenic undeveloped shoreline where eagle, osprey, and loon reside.

**Viewing Information:** From May to October expect to see bald eagle and osprey on nesting platforms, and common loon with young on their backs. Great blue heron and spotted sandpiper search the shallows and shorelines for food, while deer, muskrat, mink, and beaver make occasional appearances. In early May, watch for migrating waterfowl including mergansers. Best viewing is by boat. Excursions are available by all-weather boat from mid-May through mid-October. Call for reservations.

**Directions:** *From Hazelhurst take US 51 south. Turn right on County Hwy. Y. Turn right on Willow Dam Road to Wilderness Cruises parking lot.*

**Ownership:** Wilderness Cruises 1-800-472-1516 (for excursions); Wisconsin Valley Improvement Company (715) 848-2976
**Size:** 7,368 acres    **Closest Town:** Hazelhurst

*Sometimes you need to look "down under" to catch a glimpse of wildlife. Spotted salamanders inhabit the cool, moist floors of the northwoods finding food and shelter beneath leaves and mossy logs.* A.B. SHELDON

## 16. NICOLET NATIONAL FOREST: ANVIL TRAILS

**Description:** Anvil Trails is the oldest trail system in Wisconsin. The forest cover of white pine, hemlock, oak, and sugar maple attracts spring songbirds and northwoods mammals.

**Viewing Information:** This area's steep hillsides allow easy viewing of canopy-dwelling warblers and kinglets in the trees below. Search for scarlet tanager, gray squirrel, ruffed grouse, wood duck, white-tailed deer, and black bear in the oaks. Listen as red-eyed vireo, American redstart, ovenbird, and wood thrush search for insects. In spring, salamanders lay eggs in the shallow pools on the forest floor.

**Directions:** See map.
**Ownership:** USFS (715) 479-2827
**Size:** 1,280 acres
**Closest Town:** Eagle River

## 17. NICOLET NATIONAL FOREST: BRULE RIVER

**Description:** Not to be confused with the Bois Brule River in northwestern Wisconsin, this site is similarly a wild, remote stretch of water through the great northwoods where wildlife abounds.

**Viewing Information:** A quiet canoe trip through this secluded backcountry offers viewing of beaver, muskrat, mink, raccoon, and otter. Deer sometimes cross the shallows at twilight. Spying a black bear is a rare thrill. Wood duck, common merganser, belted kingfisher, spotted sandpiper, great blue heron, yellow warbler, and winter wren reside along the river, spring through fall. Eagle and osprey search the river for fish. Listen for spring peeper, and green and northern leopard frogs in spring and summer. Good viewing points are also accessible by remote gravel roads. Call ahead for maps, road and river conditions.

**Directions:** *From Eagle River take WI 70 east. Turn left at WI 55. Go north 5 miles to Brule River Campground.*

**Ownership:** USFS (715) 528-4464
**Size:** 30 miles of riverway
**Closest Towns:** Eagle River, WI; Iron River, MI; Florence, WI

## 18. CREX MEADOWS WILDLIFE AREA

**Description:** One of Wisconsin's premier wildlife viewing areas, this vast complex of wetlands, flowages, brush-prairie, and forests is intensively managed to support common and endangered wildlife species.

**Viewing Information:** Waterfowl arrive in late March. Some just stop for rest and refueling and others establish breeding territories. Broods of resident giant Canada geese provide enjoyable viewing in May and June. Loon, grebes, bitterns, yellow rail, sandhill crane, sedge and marsh wren, along with yellow-headed blackbird, common yellowthroat, northern harrier, LeConte's and swamp sparrow, osprey, and eagle make the wetlands their home during warm months. Also look for mink, muskrat, beaver, Blanding's turtle, chorus frog, spring peeper, Cope's gray treefrog, and salamanders. Find federally-listed endangered trumpeter swans on the flowages through summer. In April, sharp-tailed grouse stamp out mating dances in the open while Franklin's ground squirrel, pocket gopher, and badger burrow underground. Savannah, vesper, and clay-colored sparrow, upland sandpiper, prairie skink, and hognose snake are other special residents of the sand prairies. Deer, black bear, bobcat, snowshoe hare, ruffed grouse, squirrels, flycatchers, and warblers inhabit the oak, jack pine, and aspen forests. Waterfowl numbers peak in October as Canada goose, snow goose, and ducks of every sort congregate by the thousands. White pelicans are occasional spring visitors. Great gray owls migrate from Canada in extremely cold winters. Crex Meadows is easily toured by car; an excellent viewing blind. Maps, auto tour, and other information at headquarters.

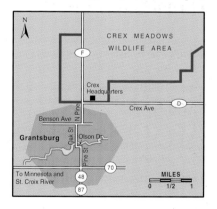

**Directions:** *See map.*

**Ownership:** WDNR (715) 463-2896
**Size:** 30,000 acres
**Closest Town:** Grantsburg

The black bear is the largest resident Wisconsin mammal. Between 6,000 and 7,000 bears inhabit Wisconsin's northwoods. These incredible hulks must meet their entire year's nutritional needs in only 6 to 8 months. They are most active mid-May through late September during which time they feed heavily on greens, nuts, berries, carrion, insects, and small mammals. In late fall, they enter their dens and fall into a deep, winter sleep, not hibernation.

# 19. ST. CROIX NATIONAL SCENIC RIVERWAY

**Description:** Recognized as one of the cleanest river systems in the country, the St. Croix and Namekagon rivers have many moods. Narrow, remote cold-water trout streams widen and flow through marshes, swamps, and bogs, and become a wide, deep river sheltered by high bluffs. Gentle banks and rugged cliffs cloaked in pines, brush, hardwoods, and pastoral farms provide habitats for a diversity of wildlife.

**Viewing Information:** Viewing is best by canoe, spring through autumn. On the rivers' upper reaches watch for black bear, bobcat, and red-shouldered hawk. Three distinct gray wolf packs have been documented along the riverway. Successful reintroduction of federally-listed endangered trumpeter swans allows a glimpse of these elegant birds. Bald eagle and osprey nest along the forested shores. Marshes are favorite haunts for wood duck, mallard, great blue heron, and kingfisher. Beaver, beaver dams, otter, mink, and muskrat are frequent sights along the waterway, as are painted and softshell turtle. The St. Croix Barrens supports sharp-tailed grouse, common yellowthroat, pocket gopher, and badger. Northern goshawks prey upon ruffed grouse in the aspen and birch woodlands. White-tailed deer are common and spend severe winters in the Kohler Peet Swamp Hardwoods and Namekagon Bottoms. Look for the tracks of the reintroduced fisher, which feed on snowshoe hare, red squirrel, and even porcupine. Three visitor centers are open seasonally in Trego, WI; in Stillwater, MN; and on MN 70. Headquarters/visitor center in St. Croix Falls is open year-round. All provide exhibits and detailed information about the area, including land access viewing opportunities. *PLEASE OBSERVE CLOSURE SIGNS FOR NESTING SITES.*

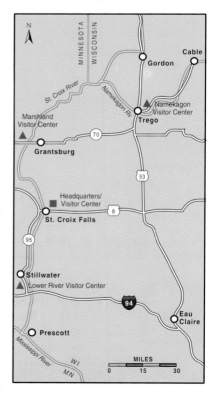

**Directions:** *Headquarters and visitor center are located at the corner of Hamilton and Massachusetts streets in St. Croix Falls. From US 8 proceed north on WI 87 for 1 mile to Massachusetts. Turn left and continue to end of block. See map.*

**Ownership:** NPS (715) 483-3284
**Size:** 252 miles of river
**Closest Town:** Trego, WI; Stillwater, MN; St. Croix Falls, WI

## 20. INTERSTATE PARK

**Description:** Rock potholes and a steep gorge formed from torrential glacial meltwaters characterize this stretch of the St. Croix National Scenic Riverway where birding is excellent.

**Viewing Information:** Turkey vulture and broad-winged and red-tailed hawk soar above the spectacular gorge, while hooded merganser splash about in the waters below. In March, eastern bluebirds arrive. May brings ovenbird, veery, wood thrush, and a host of songbirds. Look for beaver, mink, otter, and muskrat along Silverbrook Trail. Blue-spotted salamanders migrate in autumn. Look for five-lined and prairie skink and red-bellied and western fox snake in high rock outcroppings. Soft-shelled and Blanding's turtle bask in backwater sloughs. In winter, bald eagles congregate north of the park near the dam. Ice Age National Scientific Reserve Interpretive Center has exhibits, programs.

*Directions: Take US 8 east from St. Croix Falls. Take WI 35 south for 1.25 miles.*

**Ownership:** WDNR (715) 483-3747
**Size:** 1,400 acres    **Closest Town:** St. Croix Falls

*Jet black wings and tail set against a vermillion body make the scarlet tanager easy to spot high in the treetops when they arrive in Wisconsin each spring.*
A.B. SHELDON

## 21. CHEQUAMEGON NATIONAL FOREST: CHEQUAMEGON WATERS FLOWAGE

**Description:** There is easy roadside viewing of northwoods wildlife at this large flowage.

**Viewing Information:** Drive, walk, or canoe around the flowage. Late April and May bring tundra swan, Canada and snow goose, grebes, and hundreds of ducks and mergansers. Standing dead trees host wood duck. Bald eagles nest here and two areas have osprey nesting platforms. In summer, watch for double-crested cormorant, terns, green heron, common loon, and belted kingfisher, as well as otter, beaver, and muskrat. Coyotes often howl at dusk.

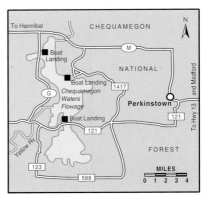

**Directions:** See map.

**Ownership:** USFS (715) 748-4875
**Size:** 2,714 acres
**Closest Town:** Perkinstown

## 22. MARATHON COUNTY FOREST: BITZKE BIRDWALK

**Description:** This waterfowl refuge hosts moderate concentrations of ducks and geese each spring.

**Viewing Information:** Wander the wetland trails for views of muskrat, mink, beaver, otter, great blue heron, and American bittern. Blue-winged teal, wood duck, mallard, and giant Canada goose abound in the flowages from mid-April to the end of May. View sandhill cranes from auto tour route. Northern harrier and kestrel search for prey. Sandpipers and killdeer probe the soft soil for invertebrates. Viewing tower and marsh boardwalks enhance the viewing experience.

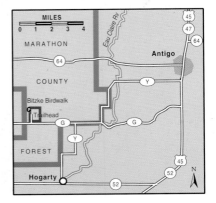

**Directions:** See map.

**Ownership:** Marathon County Forestry Department (715) 847-5267; Co-manager: WDNR (715) 627-4317
**Size:** 280 acres
**Closest Town:** Antigo

*The long, spindle legs and sharp, pointed beak of the great blue heron make this common marsh bird an efficient shallow-water predator of frogs, fish, and snakes.*
JOHN GERLACH

## 23. NICOLET NATIONAL FOREST: CATHEDRAL PINES

**Description:** This dynamic, exceptionally scenic old-growth forest is one of the few remnant stands of towering white pine and hemlock in Wisconsin to have survived the lumberjack heydays.

**Viewing Information:** In June and July, raucous sounds emanate from the

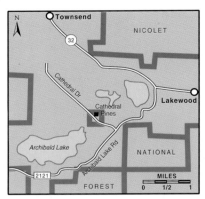

great blue heron rookery. *OBSERVE HERONS FROM RESPECTFUL DISTANCE. HUMAN PRESENCE IS DISRUPTIVE TO BIRDS.* Blackburnian, magnolia, and pine warbler and ovenbird nest here May and June. Eagles also nest nearby. Though very elusive, pine marten and fisher dart amongst the pine boughs in search of their favorite prey: porcupine, snowshoe hare, and red squirrel. Roadside parking only. *CATHEDRAL DRIVE NARROW, MAY BE IMPASSABLE IN WINTER.*

**Directions:** *See map.*

**Ownership:** USFS (715) 276-6333
**Size:** 15 acres    **Closest Town:** Lakewood

## 24. NICOLET NATIONAL FOREST: KNOWLES CREEK IMPOUNDMENT

**Description:** Adjacent to forest and grasslands, this impoundment demonstrates a wildlife marsh managed by manipulating water levels.

**Viewing Information:** From a barrier-free viewing platform and water-side trail, watch for wood duck, hooded merganser, pied-billed grebe, turkey vulture, rough-winged swallow, great blue heron, and belted kingfisher throughout spring and summer. Muskrats swim near shore as chipmunk, red squirrel, porcupine, fox, coyote, and black bear search for food on land. Look for northern harrier, bald eagle, and red-tailed hawk. Interpretive signs on trail. *ACCESS ROAD MAY BE TOTALLY IMPASSABLE IN WINTER.*

**Directions:** *From Wabeno take County Hwy. C east 9 miles. Look for Impoundment sign. Turn right on access road. Drive 0.5 mile to trail head.*

**Ownership:** USFS (715) 674-4481
**Size:** 170 acres    **Closest Town:** Wabeno

## 25. GEORGE W. MEAD WILDLIFE AREA

**Description:** A premier wildlife viewing area, Mead is known for its waterfowl and wetland birds. Berkhahn Flowage contains the state's largest human-made cormorant rookery.

**Viewing Information:** Walk the 3-mile Berkhahn Flowage Trail where beaver, mink, otter, American bittern, ring-necked duck, goldeneye, bufflehead, wood duck, blue-winged teal, and Canada goose share the area with double-crested cormorant and black-crowned night heron. Bald eagle and osprey cruise the flowage. Yellow-headed blackbirds nest in the cattails. Nearby woods yield deer, veery, and pileated woodpecker. Best viewing occurs on spring mornings and evenings, when thousands of spring peeper, pickerel, and northern leopard frog serenade. At Rice Lake Flowage watch Canada and snow goose, tundra swan, canvasback, and black duck as federally-listed endangered peregrine falcons swoop in for a meal. Reintroduced trumpeter swans frequent the flowage with black tern. During those summers when water is drawn down, stilts, phalaropes, and other shorebirds flock the mudflats. An adjacent bog is home to snowshoe hare and elusive bobcat. Smokey Hill hosts a restored tallgrass prairie where native grasses and flowers provide a backdrop for sandhill crane, badger, red fox, and bobolink. When not involved in their dawn breeding rituals on Smokey Hill in April and May, greater prairie chickens lay low to escape the keen eyes of northern harrier, rough-legged hawk, and great horned owl. *DO NOT DISTURB PRAIRIE CHICKENS DURING BREEDING; PLEASE OBSERVE AT A DISTANCE WITH VIEWING SCOPE. ACCESS ROADS MAY FLOOD IN SPRING AND FALL. SEASONAL REFUGE CLOSURES. CONTACT HEADQUARTERS FOR DATES AND CONDITIONS.*

**Directions:** *From Milladore take US 10 west. Turn right on County Hwy. S and travel north 7 miles to headquarters.*

**Ownership:** WDNR (715) 457-6771
**Size:** 28,000 acres    **Closest Town:** Milladore

*Once on the Wisconsin threatened species list, the double-crested cormorant has successfully repopulated the state. After years of a steady rebound, the species was taken off the list in 1986. Watch these ungainly birds as they sun their water-logged feathers on half-stretched wings.*

JOHN GERLACH

# REGION THREE: LAKE MICHIGAN LOWLAND

This region's coastal and inland habitats are low, moist, and dominated by sugar maple, hemlock, yellow birch, basswood, American elm, and the state's only significant example of American beech. A remnant boreal forest of balsam fir, spruce, and tamarack is found on Door County's northeastern shore; marshes, freshwater estuaries, sandy beaches, and dunes are special features of this habitat.

The Lake Michigan shoreline is an important migratory route for songbirds, shorebirds, and raptors. Assorted diving ducks, including those more commonly associated with the Atlantic Ocean, swim in the deep offshore waters. More common puddle ducks, such as mallard, blue-winged teal, and wood duck, nest in the shallow marshes. Native lake trout and introduced salmon and smelt migrate up coastal rivers to spawn. White-tailed deer, porcupine, beaver, muskrat, and red squirrel are a few of the typical mammals.

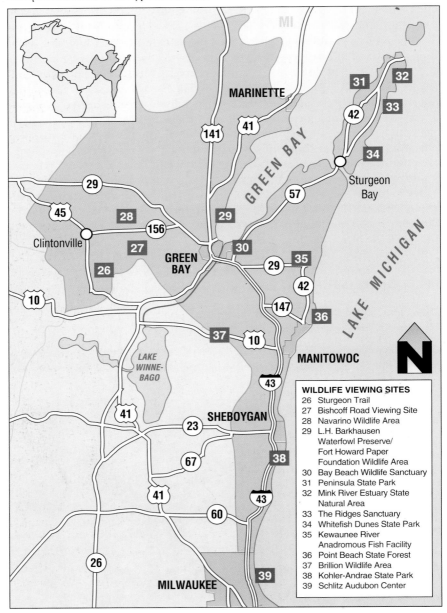

**WILDLIFE VIEWING SITES**

26  Sturgeon Trail
27  Bishcoff Road Viewing Site
28  Navarino Wildlife Area
29  L.H. Barkhausen
    Waterfowl Preserve/
    Fort Howard Paper
    Foundation Wildlife Area
30  Bay Beach Wildlife Sanctuary
31  Peninsula State Park
32  Mink River Estuary State
    Natural Area
33  The Ridges Sanctuary
34  Whitefish Dunes State Park
35  Kewaunee River
    Anadromous Fish Facility
36  Point Beach State Forest
37  Brillion Wildlife Area
38  Kohler-Andrae State Park
39  Schlitz Audubon Center

## 26. STURGEON TRAIL

**Description:** Few places on earth can boast the annual spawning of enormous lake sturgeon. The Lake Winnebago system has the world's largest single concentration of these amazing fish.

**Viewing information:** The early springtime spawning of lake sturgeon is an exciting event not to be missed. These prehistoric giants have survived to modern times and annually swim upstream from Lake Winnebago to spawn on the rocky shorelines of the Wolf and Embarrass rivers. The event is dependent on water temperature, but typically occurs for several days between late April and early May when waterflow is high. Call ahead for details.

**Directions:** *Area A: (URBAN) Pfeifer Park in New London. Take WI 45 north. Turn right onto Waupaca St., and follow to Embarrass Dr.; turn left. Go to Pfeifer Park and walk along south edge of Embarrass River. Area B: Travel about 2 miles west of New London on County Hwy. X. Park in DNR Mukwa Wildlife Area parking lot on south side of highway and walk along south edge of Wolf River. USE CAUTION ON HIGHWAY.*

**Ownership:** City of New London (Chamber of Commerce) (414) 982-5822; WDNR (414) 424-3050

**Size:** NA   **Closest Town:** New London

*The sturgeon is a huge primitive fish that cruises the bottom of rivers associated with Lake Winnebago. Females breed only once every four years after they've reached 25 years of age. The annual spawning makes one of the most spectacular wildlife watching events in the state.* RONALD M. BRUCH

## 27. BISHCOFF ROAD VIEWING SITE

**Description:** This managed wetland constitutes one of the best areas in the state to observe migrating waterfowl and shorebirds.

**Viewing Information:** These flowages transform into a birder's paradise each spring and fall as thousands of swans, geese, and ducks stop to replenish their reserves. The first migrants are tundra swans arriving in April, followed by wading birds and shorebirds, including spotted sandpiper, snipe, phalarope, plovers, and herons. A barrier-free observation mound provides easy viewing without disturbing birds.

*Directions: From Shiocton take WI 54 east 2.5 miles. Turn left (north) on Bischoff Road.*

**Ownership:** WDNR (414) 832-1804; Development: WDOT (414) 492-5712
**Size:** 481 acres    **Closest Town:** Shiocton

## 28. NAVARINO WILDLIFE AREA

**Description:** Navarino is characterized by wooded expanses interspersed with wetlands and grasslands. Active management includes logging, water-level manipulation, prescribed burning, and native plant community restoration.

**Viewing Information:** Navarino is rich in wetland wildlife, from beaver and otter, to black tern, northern harrier, and numerous ducks, herons, and grebes. Marsh edges may reveal bittern, sora, green frog, painted turtle, and fox snake. In spring, look north along Lindster Road to view thousands of brilliant white tundra swans, Canada geese, and sandhill cranes. Trails leading from McDonald Road end at flowages where hooded merganser, bufflehead, goldeneye, pintail, northern shoveler, wood duck, blue-winged teal, ring-necked duck, and scaup are present. In the forests, catch glimpses of ruffed grouse, American woodcock, ovenbird, white-tailed deer, snowshoe hare, pileated woodpecker, and barred owl. Eastern bluebird, ground squirrel, meadowlark, American kestrel, and grasshopper sparrow inhabit the grasslands. Nature center offers a self-guided trail with boardwalk, and occasional programs.

**Directions:** See map.

**Ownership:** WDNR (715) 524-2183; Navarino Nature Center (pvt) (715) 524-2297
**Size:** 14,500 acres
**Closest Town:** Navarino

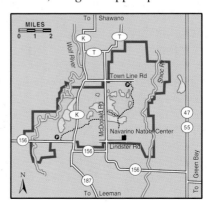

## 29. L.H. BARKHAUSEN WATERFOWL PRESERVE/ FORT HOWARD PAPER FOUNDATION WILDLIFE AREA

**Description:** Sitting at the southern end of the once-vast Green Bay west shore wetland-prairie complex, this preserve supports diverse wildlife communities associated with marsh, shrublands, lowland woods, and a tiny remnant of prairie.

**Viewing Information:** Thousands of ducks, geese, and tundra swans stop along the shores of Green Bay to feed and rest during spring and fall migrations. Resident giant Canada geese provide year-round viewing. Spend the day exploring trails where deer, fox, and coyote may be seen. A host of song, shore, and wading birds, including sora and Virginia rail, black-crowned night heron, least bittern, and common and snowy egret set up household in wetlands. During warm spring evenings listen to spring peeper, wood and tree frog, and bullfrog as big brown and little brown bat dart about overhead. In winter, listen for the calls of great horned and barred owl. West Shores Interpretive Center offers exhibits and naturalist programs. *PLEASE STAY ON MARKED TRAILS AND RESPECT AREA CLOSURES.*

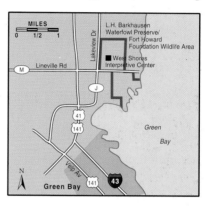

**Directions:** *See map.*

**Ownership:** Brown County (414) 434-2824
**Size:** 920 acres    **Closest Town:** Green Bay

**LAKE MICHIGAN LOWLAND**

*Western painted turtles are commonly seen basking on submerged logs near the banks of ponds and small lakes in northern Wisconsin. Approach slowly and quietly for a better view.* A.B. SHELDON

## 30. BAY BEACH WILDLIFE SANCTUARY

**Description:** URBAN SITE. A model urban wildlife refuge, Bay Beach provides a place where people can interact with wildlife through educational and recreational activities.

**Viewing Information:** Explore the center's multi-level exhibits and experience how habitats and succession affect the area's wildlife. View an eagle at its nest atop a tall white pine tree, eavesdrop on a conversation between fire rangers in a fire tower, and whirl down a tube slide for an "underwater" look at a beaver pond. At the indoor Wildlife Observation Deck, watch birds and other wildlife through one-way glass with sound piped in from outside. Journey along trails through forest, field, and marsh. The Woodland Community Building exhibits some of Wisconsin's more elusive creatures including red fox, gray fox, gray wolf, and white-tailed deer. The lagoon and surrounding area support a substantial waterfowl flock, including giant Canada goose, pintail, gadwall, wood duck, mallard, and teal. Programs are regularly scheduled.

*Directions: In Green Bay, take I-43 north to exit 187 (Webster Ave.), turn right at bottom of ramp onto Webster Ave. Travel 2 blocks to Irwin Ave. intersection. Follow sign to Sanctuary, 4 blocks ahead.*

**Ownership:** City of Green Bay  (414) 391-3675
**Size:** 700 acres    **Closest Town:** Green Bay

*White-tailed deer were voted Wisconsin's most popular wildlife to watch. Look for signs of deer in areas where forest meets field: hoof prints in mud or snow, well-worn trails, antler rubs on saplings, scrapes beneath small trees, pellets, and bedding sites.*

MARK S. WERNER

## 31. PENINSULA STATE PARK

**Description:** On Door Peninsula's western shore, this park boasts high cliffs, cobble beaches, beech-maple climax forests, paper birch, and white cedar forests.

**Viewing Information:** In hardwood forests look for pileated woodpecker. Severely gnawed bark at the base of trees and "browse lines" in the white cedar stands are signs of high deer populations. The open water, sedge meadows, and mixed conifer forests at Weborg Point are great places to seek frogs and waterbirds. Herring and ring-billed gull, cormorant, terns, and shorebirds inhabit the Green Bay shores. In winter look for saw-whet and snowy owl, goshawk, evening grosbeak, redpoll, and pine siskin. Seasonal naturalist programs.

*Directions: From Fish Creek travel 0.5 mile north on WI 42. Entrance on west side of road.*

**Ownership:** WDNR (414) 868-3258
**Size:** 3,763 acres    **Closest Town:** Fish Creek

## 32. MINK RIVER ESTUARY STATE NATURAL AREA

**Description:** This pristine estuary is an important fish spawning ground and a critical migration area for more than 200 species of birds.

**Viewing Information:** This sensitive wetland ecosystem of deep marshes, sedge meadows, and cedar-hemlock and hardwood forests is best viewed by canoe, spring through fall. Watch for beaver, mergansers, black tern, black-crowned night heron, American bittern, common loon, double-crested cormorant, northern harrier, and sedge and marsh wren. Trails meander through a boreal forest where coyote, black bear, snowshoe hare, and porcupine thrive. Boat launch (fee), canoe rentals, and boat excursions available at nearby Wagon Trail Resort (414) 854-2385.

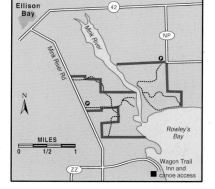

*Directions: See map.*

**Ownership:** TNC (608) 251-8140
**Size:** 1,151 acres    **Closest Town:** Ellison Bay

## 33. THE RIDGES SANCTUARY

**Description:** This Door County sanctuary features a remnant boreal (northern) forest, typical of those found along Lake Superior. Complete with ancient shoreline ridges, acidic-water swales, and Lake Michigan beach, this is a delicate, unusual, and complex community of rare wildflowers and northwoods wildlife.

**Viewing Information:** More than 25 native orchids and other rare wildflowers bloom from late April to mid-October. Step into spruce, hemlock, and balsam fir stands and listen to noisy red squirrels chatter as hairy, downy, and pileated woodpeckers drum on dead trees. Sharp-shinned hawk, saw-whet owl, raven, red-breasted nuthatch, winter wren, northern waterthrush, wood thrush, and a variety of warblers (including the Nashville, black-throated green, and Blackburnian) make this site a temporary home. Snowshoe hare and white-tailed deer are seen here. Watch for fox dens along the sandy ridges, and spotted sandpiper, killdeer, and herring gull on the beach. From November through April, scan the beach for oldsquaw, common goldeneye, bufflehead, and red-breasted merganser. In summer, Caspian tern patrols the skies along the lakeshore. Interpretive center and tours, May through October.

*Directions: From Baileys Harbor take WI 57 north. Turn right on County Hwy. Q and take first driveway on right.*

**Ownership:** The Ridges Sanctuary, Inc. (414) 839-2802
**Size:** 1,200 acres    **Closest Town:** Baileys Harbor

### SLIP SLIDING AWAY

Some of the best wildlife viewing in Wisconsin is done on the water. Animals are less afraid of a canoe or boat drifting by than they are of humans on foot. When you spot a heron or bittern, a brood of ducks, or a playful otter, turn off your boat's engine or stop paddling your canoe, crouch low, use your paddle as a rudder, and let the currents slip you in for a close glimpse.

**Description:** Sitting on Door County Peninsula's eastern shore, this park boasts fragile dune communities, the highest sand dune in the state, plus shorebirds, songbirds, and northwoods mammals.

**Viewing Information:** The beach is excellent for viewing herring and ring-billed gull and spotted sandpiper in summer and Bonaparte's gull and common and Caspian tern in spring and fall. In winter, snowshoe hare put on coats of white, while hairy and downy woodpecker, tree sparrow, dark-eyed junco, chickadee, and an occasional snowy owl stop to visit. All through winter, diving ducks such as bufflehead and goldeneye can be seen from the nature center deck. Typical park mammals include white-tailed deer, red fox, porcupine, red squirrel, and raccoon. Mink and fisher are elusive residents. Evidence of the pileated woodpecker can be seen throughout the hardwood forests. Nature center has maps, exhibits, and seasonal programs. *PLEASE STAY ON DUNE CORDWALKS.*

**Directions:** *Take WI 57 north from Sturgeon Bay. Proceed 1 mile past Valmy. Take first right onto Clark Lake Road; go 3 miles to entrance.*

**Ownership:** WDNR (414) 823-2400
**Size:** 867 acres     **Closest Town:** Valmy

**LAKE MICHIGAN LOWLAND**

*Whitefish Dunes State Park has the highest sand dunes on Lake Michigan's western shore. Four threatened species, including the dune thistle and dune goldenrod, can be found in this unusual wind-blown habitat.* DARRYL R. BEERS

*The red fox is a common predator of forest and field, combing farm country in search of rabbits, mice, and meadow voles. Watch them as they stalk their prey. In winter, look for this carnivore sunning itself on southern slopes of hills.*
BARBARA GERLACH

## 35. KEWAUNEE RIVER ANADROMOUS FISH FACILITY

**Description:** Chinook and coho salmon and rainbow trout are held in this facility temporarily for egg collection during their upstream spawning migrations. Eggs collected from these anadromous fish are taken to WDNR hatcheries where they hatch and grow until they are stocked into Lake Michigan tributaries.

**Viewing Information:** From the barrier-free observation deck and paved walkway, follow the fish from the fish barrier through the fish ladder to large holding ponds. During the runs, watch hundreds of large fish splashing and jumping up the fish ladder. At an underwater window, peer through murky waters for a fish-eye view of the action. Rainbow trout spawning runs peak in April and July through August. Brown trout runs are in late September through November. Chinook and coho salmon runs peak in October, extending into November.

*Directions: From Kewaunee travel west on WI 29. Turn off and continue west on County Hwy. C for 1.5 miles. Turn left on County Hwy. F and go 0.5 mile to Ransom Moore Lane along Kewaunee River. Turn right into facility.*

**Ownership:** WDNR (414) 388-1025
**Size:** 10 acres    **Closest Town:** Kewaunee

## 36. POINT BEACH STATE FOREST

**Description:** Part of a major migration corridor along scenic Lake Michigan, this site offers forests of hemlock, pine, and northern hardwoods, and beach, dunes, ridges, and swales that provide habitat for songbirds and shorebirds.

**Viewing information:** Spring migration brings a host of vireos and warblers. Whip-poor-wills serenade in late May. Gulls and terns patrol the skies as sandpipers and upland plover comb the dunes. Little brown bats emerge at dusk. White-tailed deer, red and gray fox, mink, and thirteen-lined ground squirrel are common. Molash Creek shelters great blue heron. Exhibits, interpretive nature trail and boardwalk.

*Directions: From Two Rivers take WI 42 north. Turn right on Viceroy Road. Turn left (north) on County Hwy. O. Nature Center is 4 miles on right.*

**Ownership:** WDNR (414) 794-7480
**Size:** 3,200 acres    **Closest town:** Two Rivers

**LAKE MICHIGAN LOWLAND**

Luna Moth

White Pine

Barred Owl

Northern
Flying Squirrel

Sugar Maple

White Birch

Balsam Fir

Black Bear

Goshawk

Yellow Birch

White-tailed Deer
(in velvet)

Currant

Red-headed Woodpecker

Porcupine

Trillium

Bobcat

Snowshoe Hare

Ruffed Grouse

Bracken Fungus

Red-backed Salamander

Bunchberry

Fox Snake

Ovenbird

# FORESTS: MORE THAN JUST TREES

Forests are more than just trees. They are a complex community of plants and animals that constantly change, grow, and interact with each other and the nutrient-bearing soils upon which they depend. Once, more than half of Wisconsin was cloaked in vast stretches of forest: maple woodlands, spruce and pine groves, oak savannas, river-bottom thickets, and more. But the axe, the plow, and the bulldozer have changed that landscape into a patchwork quilt of forest fragmented by towns, fields, and roads. Some forest wildlife depend on the interior of large unbroken tracts, others prefer living at forest's edge. Some wildlife need young forests, others require mature, or "old-growth," forests to survive.

## 37. BRILLION WILDLIFE AREA

**Description:** This site, located on a floodplain at the confluence of Spring Creek and Manitowoc River, provides excellent viewing of wetland, grassland, and forest wildlife.

**Viewing information:** View common mammals year-round including white-tailed deer, red fox, muskrat, mink, and raccoon. Blue-winged teal, mallard, wood duck, great blue heron, yellow-headed blackbird, and Canada goose seek out the wetlands and open water. Grasshopper sparrow, sandhill crane, bobo-link, and northern harrier prefer the grasslands. Prairie wildflower display peaks mid-summer. In winter look for short-eared owl and rough-legged hawk. Ruffed grouse and bald eagle may also be seen. Snapping turtle and wood frog are common. A privately operated nature center, open in summer, offers displays. Trails open year-round.

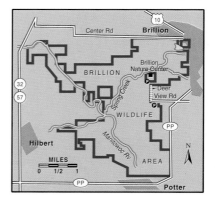

**Directions:** *See map.*

**Ownership:** WDNR (414) 832-1804
**Size:** 4,762 acres
**Closest town:** Brillion

## WILDLIFE WATCHING FOR INSOMNIACS

Some animals can best be seen or heard at night. Great horned owls hoot, barred owls query "who cooks for you, who cooks for you, all," and screech owls quaver. Bats and flying squirrels are very active after sundown. Check your porch light, street lamp, or shine a flashlight against an old white sheet to attract moths, June bugs, and a host of other invertebrates. On cool spring evenings, listen for the unusual mating ritual of the woodcock. As the weather warms, listen for whip-poor-wills, nighthawks, spring peepers, and toads. Coyotes and wolves howl at night; red foxes yelp. Since animals typically cannot detect red light, take along a flashlight with its lens wrapped in red cellophane. Shine the light across fields, marshes, and forests to catch the flicker of "eye shine." Contact Wisconsin DNR for laws regarding "shining."

## 38. KOHLER-ANDRAE STATE PARK

**Description:** From the marshes along the Black River to the sandy beaches, rolling dunes, and beech/white pine forest, this park offers excellent viewing of migrating waterfowl, hawks, and songbirds.

**Viewing Information:** In spring and fall, impressive numbers of diving ducks like scaup, common goldeneye, bufflehead, and mergansers drift just offshore of this important migratory corridor. Each summer, spectacular hatches of blue and green darner dragonflies attract large flocks of nighthawks and ring-billed and herring gull. Likewise, in June and late July the annual die-off of alewives, a type of herring, attracts gulls, raccoon, fox, and skunk. Sandhill cranes nest in marshes, where Canada goose, green-winged teal, wood duck, great blue heron, sora rail, and kingfisher seek shelter. Woodlands support wrens, wood thrush, and numerous warblers, especially in migration. White-tailed deer live in the park, as do mink, muskrat, and squirrels. River otter, beaver, coyote, and badger are present. The state natural area harbors a number of rare and threatened plant species. Sanderling Nature Center contains displays. *PLEASE STAY ON DUNE CORDWALKS.*

**Directions:** *From Sheboygan take I-43 south. Take County Hwy. V exit. Go 1 mile east. Turn right on County Hwy. KK. Go 1 mile. Turn left on Old Park Road into park.*

**Ownership:** WDNR (414) 452-3457
**Size:** 1,000 acres    **Closest Town:** Sheboygan

**LAKE MICHIGAN LOWLAND**

*An adult green darner dragonfly emerges from its crusty and cramped body shell it wore as a nymph. While in a nymphal stage, these wetland insects feed on tadpoles underwater. As adults, they become aerial pond predators feasting on mosquitoes, gnats, and other small insects. These dragonflies migrate south in late September.*

DARRYL R. BEERS

# 39. SCHLITZ AUDUBON CENTER

**Description:** URBAN SITE. Close to Milwaukee, this sanctuary is located along the Lake Michigan shore. It includes beach, bluff, ravine, hardwood forest, meadow, and pond wildlife communities.

**Viewing Information:** A 60-foot treetop classroom offers a panoramic perspective of the lake and its wooded bluffs. More than 250 species of birds are sighted annually at the center, located on an important migratory corridor. During spring and fall, scan the lake for diving ducks including redhead, ring-necked duck, common goldeneye, and oldsquaw. Yellowlegs, ruddy turnstone, and pectoral sandpipers also migrate through. Endangered and threatened species such as peregrine falcon, bald eagle, osprey, and Forster's terns frequent this property. Indigo bunting and kingbird nest here. Red fox hunt rabbits, while red squirrels find safety in spruce trees along the ravines. The habits of white-tailed deer are interpreted along barrier-free Green Trail. Along the Boardwalk Pond Trail, watch for Blanding's and painted turtle. Watch wetland birds from the wildlife blind on the meadow's south pond. Raccoon, deer, and muskrat tracks in mud. Nature center has displays and programs.

**Directions:** *From Milwaukee take I-43 north to Brown Deer Road exit. Go east about 1 mile to nature center.*

**Ownership:** National Audubon Society (414) 352-2880
**Size:** 225 acres      **Closest Town:** Bayside

*The prominent white band ringing the bill, and the black back and chest with white belly cresting up in front of the wing help identify the ring-necked duck. Watch the shores of Lake Michigan for these divers as they rest and refuel during migration.*

JOHN GERLACH

## REGION FOUR: WESTERN DRIFTLESS UPLAND

Continental glaciers scoured most of Wisconsin, but missed its southwestern area. Millions of years of stream carving sculpted the bedrock into rugged valleys and majestic bluffs. Southern hardwood forests of sugar maple, white oak, and aspen run downslope to mix with bottomland forests of silver maple, American elm, river birch, green ash, and swamp white oak.

This wooded landscape supports wild turkey, red-headed and pileated woodpecker, white-tailed deer, and gray and fox squirrel by day; night brings forth the barred and great horned owl, raccoon, opossum, and whip-poor-will. The dry bluffs and upland prairies are home to the badger, white-tailed jackrabbit, meadowlark, and timber rattlesnake. Fast-flowing streams support native brook trout, while the sluggish Mississippi River serves as a major flyway for waterfowl, most notably tundra swan and canvasback duck.

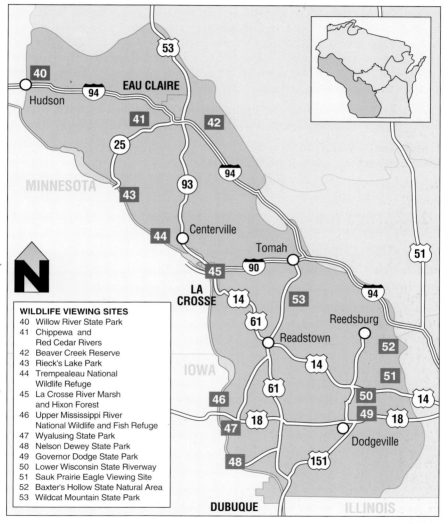

**WILDLIFE VIEWING SITES**
40  Willow River State Park
41  Chippewa and
    Red Cedar Rivers
42  Beaver Creek Reserve
43  Rieck's Lake Park
44  Trempealeau National
    Wildlife Refuge
45  La Crosse River Marsh
    and Hixon Forest
46  Upper Mississippi River
    National Wildlife and Fish Refuge
47  Wyalusing State Park
48  Nelson Dewey State Park
49  Governor Dodge State Park
50  Lower Wisconsin State Riverway
51  Sauk Prairie Eagle Viewing Site
52  Baxter's Hollow State Natural Area
53  Wildcat Mountain State Park

## 40. WILLOW RIVER STATE PARK

**Description:** A finger of tallgrass prairie reaches into Wisconsin at this site of the former Hudson Prairie, allowing some unusual prairie wildlife to reside here.

**Viewing information:** In oak-prairie landscapes, pocket gopher, white-tailed jackrabbit, prairie ring-necked snake, the prairie race of horned lark, prairie skink, and bobolink provide feasts for hungry badger, red fox, and northern harrier. Beaver, otter, false map turtle, and wood frog inhabit wetlands. The hardwood forests are home to Cooper's, red-shouldered, and broad-winged hawk, ruffed grouse, black-billed cuckoo, red-bellied woodpecker, and red-backed salamander. Migrating waterfowl find a secluded haven on two lakes in spring and fall. Watch for white-tailed deer at dusk. Hidden Ponds Nature Trail is barrier free. Nature Center offers displays and summer programs.

*Directions: From Hudson take I-94 east to exit 4. Go north on US 12. When US 12 turns sharply east, continue north to County Hwy. A. Go 1.5 miles to park entrance.*

**Ownership:** WDNR (715) 386-5931
**Size:** 2,800 acres    **Closest town:** Hudson

## 41. CHIPPEWA AND RED CEDAR RIVERS

**Description:** Forested shores of two scenic rivers are home to abundant wildlife.

**Viewing information:** View wildlife by canoe or bike. Spring and summer offer chances to see bald eagle, osprey, red-shouldered hawk, and bank swallow. Watch broods of wood ducks near shore and spotted sandpiper, great blue and green heron, and painted turtle. Explore the exceptional oak barrens and floodplain forest which support a rich diversity of plants and animals. State trails running parallel to the rivers offer views of bottomland forest. Canoe and bike rentals available in Eau Claire and Menomonie. Contact site owners for details.

*Directions: See map.*

**Ownership:** Dunn County (715) 232-1496; WDNR (715) 232-1496
**Size:** 40 mile stretch of river
**Closest town:** Eau Claire, Menomonie

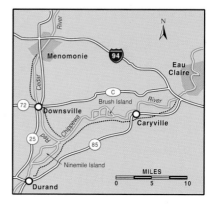

## 42. BEAVER CREEK RESERVE

**Description:** Northern pine forest meets lowland prairie here where the Eau Claire River, two trout streams, pothole ponds, alder-willow swamps, and bur oak-jack pine uplands allow views of wetland and woodland wildlife.

**Viewing Information:** March through May, listen for spring peeper, wood frog, and American woodcock along Marsh Loop. Look for skink, tiger salamander, the threatened Blanding's turtle, wood turtle, and green heron. Beaver, river otter, muskrat, and mink gambol along streambanks. As weather warms, wild turkeys gobble and ruffed grouse drum. In mid-summer, chipmunks scurry for nuts by day while little brown bats swoop for moths, and coyotes howl by night. The woodlands are alive year-round with deer, raccoon, opossum, and red squirrel. An unusual resident this far north is the tufted titmouse. Birds of prey include northern goshawk, sharp-shinned and broad-winged hawk, turkey vulture, and saw-whet owl. Black bears roam autumn woods as brook trout breed. Winter brings bald eagle and crossbills. The Wise Nature Center has programs and exhibits. Blinds and boardwalks enhance viewing.

*Directions: From Fall Creek go 4 miles north on County Hwy. K. Turn right into nature center parking lot.*

**Ownership:** Eau Claire County (715) 877-2212
**Size:** 360 acres    **Closest Town:** Fall Creek

**WESTERN DRIFTLESS**

*The tufted titmouse is an unusual resident for Wisconsin, but may be seen at the far north Beaver Creek Reserve site.* JOHN GERLACH

**Description:** Rieck's Lake Park sits at the confluence of the Buffalo and Mississippi rivers. It is noted for the impressive fall concentration of tundra swans and other waterfowl that find a haven on the waters of the Upper Mississippi River National Wildlife and Fish Refuge.

**Viewing information:** Peak viewing season for tundra swans is late October and early November when the flock builds to 2,500. Almost every kind of waterfowl common to the Mississippi Flyway, as well as herons, bitterns, and great egret, can be viewed spring and fall. The lake is dotted with muskrat huts. Mink and beaver are common. Bald eagles may be seen year-round, but particularly in winter. A barrier-free observation deck enhances viewing.

*Directions: From Alma go 1 mile north on WI 35. Proceed past WI 37 intersection. Park entrance is on left.*

**Ownership:** City of Alma (608) 685-3330; ACE; USFWS
**Size:** 12 acres    **Closest town:** Alma

*Late October to early November is the peak viewing season to watch nearly 2,500 tundra swans migrating through Rieck's Lake Park, a popular stopover on the Mississippi Flyway.* A.B. SHELDON

# 44. TREMPEALEAU NATIONAL WILDLIFE REFUGE

**Description:** The Mississippi and Trempealeau rivers bound this refuge whose clean backwaters, marshes, hardwood forests, and sand prairies provide habitat for migratory birds and upland wildlife.

**Viewing information:** A self-guided auto tour offers excellent opportunities to view wildlife. Drive past ancient sand dunes and beautiful prairies where savannah sparrow and eastern meadowlark sing, and eastern bluebirds set up house in nest boxes each spring. Enjoy barrier-free Prairie View Trail. White-tailed deer browse in nearby fields. A marsh observation deck offers views of muskrat, beaver, herons, bitterns, egret, black tern, and double-crested cormorant. During spring and fall migration, the waters along Pine Creek Dike hold concentrations of mallard, wood duck, Canada goose, and tundra swan. Osprey, northern harrier, and bald eagle nest here. Hike the wildlife interpretive trail; many songbirds and woodpeckers thrive here. Stop by secluded woodland potholes and listen for northern leopard frog or watch for painted turtle. Search for rare red-shouldered hawk in floodplain forests, or unusual black-phase gray squirrel in oak woods. The Great River State Trail is open to bicycles. *ACCESS ROAD OCCASIONALLY IMPASSABLE DUE TO FLOODING.*

*Directions: See map.*

**Ownership:** USFWS (608) 539-2311
**Size:** 5,617 acres
**Closest town:** Trempealeau

The Wisconsin Waterfowl Stamp is a great way to help ensure a bright future for the state's wetland wildlife. All proceeds from the sales of these stamps are used entirely for habitat restoration and protection projects that benefit not only ducks and geese but a great diversity of wetland and grassland wildlife as well. Stamps may be purchased at most sporting goods stores across the state or any WDNR office.

WESTERN DRIFTLESS

**Description:** URBAN SITE. Nestled among Mississippi River bluffs, Hixon Forest supports beautiful hardwood forests and native dry prairies alive with songbirds. At the bluff's base lies La Crosse River Marsh, a unique and prime urban wetland filled with waterfowl and wading birds.

**Viewing information:** The 6-mile Bicentennial Trail travels along a steep bluff-side or "goat" prairie, down through Hixon Forest, across the La Crosse River Marsh to the banks of the Mississippi. The prairie and forest sustain western meadowlark, thirteen-lined ground squirrel, woodchuck, wood thrush, eastern wood-pewee, white-tailed deer, red fox, and other common mammals. The marsh is filled with Canada goose, mallard, coot, herons, and common egret, along with muskrat, beaver, mink, frogs, and toads. Summer residents include black tern, yellow-headed blackbird, and sora, Virginia, and king rail. Bald eagles occasionally soar above while endangered peregrine falcons make a rare showing. The nature center has live animal exhibits, displays, and programs.

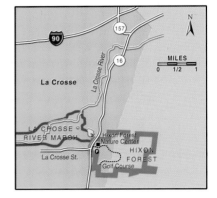

*Directions:* See map.

**Ownership:** City of La Crosse (608) 789-7533; Management: Hixon Forest Nature Center (608) 784-0303
**Size:** 1,100 acres
**Closest town:** La Crosse

*The American white pelican, an unusual bird for Wisconsin, has been increasingly seen along the Mississippi River near La Crosse. These large birds feed in groups, herding schools of fish into shallow areas where they can be scooped up in the pelicans' long bills and expandable pouches.* A.B. SHELDON

## 46. UPPER MISSISSIPPI RIVER NATIONAL WILDLIFE AND FISH REFUGE

**Description:** The boundaries of this refuge extend hundreds of miles along the Mississippi River, from just below Pepin to south of the Illinois border. This major migratory route embraces thousands of acres of wooded islands, sandbars, open waters, backwaters, and marshes.

**Viewing information:** Witness spectacular seasonal flights of waterfowl. Thousands of tundra swans stop here in the spring. Ducks, geese, bitterns, rails, and shorebirds thrive in this refuge. Large heron and egret rookeries are astir with activity during spring and early summer. *PLEASE OBSERVE ROOKERIES FROM A RESPECTFUL DISTANCE.* Beaver, river otter, muskrat, mink, raccoon, white-tailed deer, and fox are common inhabitants. In spring, warblers, vireos, and thrushes drift through the forested islands and bluffs. Pileated woodpecker, and great horned and barred owl call from deep woods. July's explosive mayfly hatch provides food for swallows and nighthawks. In October, up to 75 percent of the entire continental population of canvasback duck may be seen near LaCrosse. Lesser scaup, ring-necked duck, common goldeneye, and merganser gather in deeper water above the dams, while mallard, wigeon, gadwall, teal, and wood duck settle in the shallow backwaters. White pelicans, a rarity in the state, have been increasingly seen each summer around pools 4 through 8. Bald eagles nest and winter in the area. Scenic vistas of the river may be glimpsed from waysides along the Great River Road, WI 35, especially those at Onalaska and between Stoddard and Genoa. Excursions and boat rentals available at riverside facilities. District offices in Winona, MN (Refuge hdqtrs.); LaCrosse, WI; McGregor, IA; and Savannah, IL can provide information. Main visitor contact station in McGregor also has exhibits.

*Directions: Main visitor center is located across the river from Prairie du Chien on US 18, McGregor, IA.*

**Ownership:** USFWS (319) 873-3423; ACE (612) 290-5676
**Size:** 200,000 acres, 260 miles of riverway
**Closest town:** McGregor, Iowa

WESTERN DRIFTLESS

**Description:** Noted for its wild turkey, bald eagle, and rugged, scenic hills surrounding the confluence of the Wisconsin and Mississippi rivers, Wyalusing's trails traverse southern hardwood forests, river bottom lowlands, and steep hillsides.

**Viewing information:** Resident bald eagle and turkey vulture soar over panoramic vistas of the river valley. Once extirpated, the reintroduced wild turkey now flourishes in the park along with white-tailed deer, raccoon, and pileated and red-headed woodpecker. Hognose, fox, and black rat snakes are elusive residents. Red-tailed, broad-winged, and red-shouldered hawk, and great horned owl are typical. A canoe trail through the river sloughs offers a unique way to see herons, egret, muskrat, beaver, and mink. Mallard, teal, wood duck, and Canada goose can be seen from the boat landing and fishing pier on Glen Lake, a backwater of the Mississippi River. Don't miss the early spring floral display when the shaded cliffs are covered with shooting stars and dozens of other species. Summer naturalist programs and nature center exhibits enhance the visit.

**Directions:** *From Prairie du Chien take US 18 east 5 miles. Turn south on County Hwy. C. Turn right (west) onto County Hwy. CX. Go 1 mile to park entrance.*

**Ownership:** WDNR (608) 996-2261
**Size:** 2,700 acres   **Closest town:** Prairie du Chien

*Listen for the "gobbling" of courting wild turkeys as males stretch and strut for hens each spring. Once extirpated from the state, this largest of Wisconsin's game birds was reintroduced in 1976 through financial aid of hunters.*

MARK S. WERNER

## 48. NELSON DEWEY STATE PARK

**Description:** The Mississippi River provides excellent opportunities to view bald eagles in winter. Native bluff prairies attract a host of butterflies.

**Viewing information:** Wintering bald eagles search for fish in the warm water discharges of two Cassville power plants. These discharges keep this stretch of river flowing even in the coldest winters. Contact park for eagle-viewing information. From the native dry prairie bluffs watch migrating raptors, spring and fall. May brings Kentucky warbler, thrushes, and vireos. Wild turkey and white-tailed deer are common. Self-guided nature trail.

*Directions: From Cassville take WI 133 north. Turn left onto County Hwy. VV. Park is 1 mile on right.*

**Ownership:** WDNR (608) 725-5374
**Size:** 750 acres
**Closest town:** Cassville

## 49. GOVERNOR DODGE STATE PARK

**Description:** In the heart of unglaciated country, this park provides wildlife with a refuge in its hardwood forests, sandstone cliffs, and artificial lakes.

**Viewing information:** Watch white-tailed deer in fields and beaver on lakes. Coyote, raccoon, whip-poor-will, and barred owl provide night viewing. In springtime woods, listen for ruffed grouse, wild turkey, pileated woodpecker, and the endangered Blanchard's cricket frog. Great blue heron and wood duck are common. Look for badger and woodchuck in grasslands, where thirteen-lined ground squirrels dart for burrows as red and gray fox ready to pounce. Eastern bluebird, red-tailed hawk, and turkey vulture also present. In winter, watch river otter play on lake ice. Self-guiding trails and summer programs.

*Directions: From Dodgeville go 3 miles north on WI 23 to the park entrance on right.*

**Ownership:** WDNR  (608) 935-2315
**Size:**  5,029 acres
**Closest town:**  Dodgeville

## WETLANDS: WONDERLANDS NOT WASTELANDS

Early explorers called Wisconsin "the Great Swamp," since the territory was covered with ten million acres of wetlands—lands where water stands for at least part of the year. Wetland ecosystems are extremely valuable to wildlife, supporting a greater number of animals than any other type of habitat. Wetlands also absorb flood waters; filter chemicals, sediments, and other impurities out of drinking water; recharge groundwater; and provide a variety of recreational opportunities. Fifty percent of Wisconsin's original wetlands have disappeared. Not only must we maintain our existing wetlands, we must continue efforts to restore those that have been lost.

Osprey

Common
Yellowthroat

Aspen

Willow

Alder

Beaver

Mink

Otter

Wood Duck

Great Blue Heron

Cattails

Tiger
Salamander

Chorus Frog

Muskrat Lodge

Muskellunge

Red-winged
Blackbird

Blanding's Turtle

Reed

Lotus

Dragonfly

Arrowhead

Hellgrammite

Coontail

# 50. LOWER WISCONSIN STATE RIVERWAY

**Description:** The Wisconsin River, with more hydroelectric dams than any other river in the nation, drains over a third of the state. Below the last dam at Prairie du Sac, this "hardest working river in the nation" turns into a wild and pristine waterway slowly winding through 92 miles of rough, unglaciated terrain. This longest free-flowing stretch of river in the Midwest contains a diversity of wildlife including 62 species that are rare, threatened, or endangered.

**Viewing information:** Bald eagles hunt along the river and winter-roost among steep limestone cliffs. Spring through fall look for red-shouldered hawk, bobolink, Acadian flycatcher, Henslow's sparrow, upland sandpiper, yellow-headed blackbird, and osprey. Cerulean and prothonotary warbler, winter wren, brown creeper, and pileated and red-headed woodpecker nest here. Common loon, peregrine falcon, and chestnut-sided warbler migrate through each spring. Rare lark sparrow and ornate box turtle nest in sandy oak barrens. Ruffed grouse, bobwhite quail, wild turkey, American woodcock, white-tailed deer, gray and red fox, and coyote inhabit the woodlands. If canoeing, keep a sharp lookout for beaver, muskrat, mink, heron, and egret. Tundra swans fly overhead during late October when backwater sloughs fill with wood duck, ring-necked duck, pintail, and Canada goose. Though best viewing is by canoe, wildlife areas provide on-shore viewing. For further information contact WDNR offices. *CAUTION: WATERS CAN RISE FAST. SPECIAL REGULATIONS IN EFFECT FOR WATERCRAFT.*

**Directions:** *From Spring Green take U.S. 14 east. Turn right on County Hwy. C. Tower Hill State Park entrance is on right. See map.*

**Ownership:** WDNR (608) 935-3368; Tower Hill State Park (608) 588-2116
**Size:** 77,314 acres
**Closest town:** Spring Green

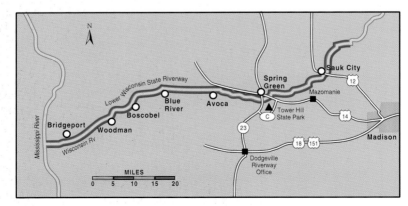

# 51. SAUK PRAIRIE EAGLE VIEWING SITE

**Description:** URBAN SITE. Bald eagles congregate each winter in the Sauk City-Prairie du Sac area.

**Viewing information:** As many as 200 bald eagles spend mid-December through mid-February along the lower Wisconsin River. Fish are plentiful here in the open waters below the river's last dam. This site features a large barrier-free observation platform, equipped with permanent spotting scope. On weekends during peak eagle-viewing period, volunteers provide interpretive information, and guidance to other nearby viewing sites. Eagles most active during morning hours. Site less crowded on weekdays. *EXCEPT AT VIEWING PLATFORM, PLEASE STAY IN VEHICLE WHILE OBSERVING EAGLES.*

*Directions: Near Sauk City take US 12 north across Wisconsin River. Turn right immediately on Water Street. Go 1.4 miles to public parking lot near Fire House Restaurant in Prairie du Sac.*

**Ownership:** Village of Prairie du Sac; Management: Ferry Bluff Eagle Council (608) 643-4168; WDNR (608) 266-7012

**Size:** 0.25 acre    **Closest town:** Prairie du Sac

*Keep an eye out for bald eagles along the Wisconsin River. The white head and tail make the adult unmistakable. Look for mottled brown and white on immature birds.*

HERBERT LANGE

**WESTERN DRIFTLESS**

## 52. BAXTER'S HOLLOW STATE NATURAL AREA

**Description:** Considered one of the most important nesting areas for forest birds in southern Wisconsin, Baxter's Hollow lies deep in the heart of the Baraboo Range. From the state's only undeveloped watershed, a quaint trout stream bubbles over boulders through hardwoods, majestic pines, and relic hemlocks where a variety of forest and aquatic wildlife flourishes.

**Viewing information:** Cooper's and broad-winged hawk and turkey vulture can be viewed during spring and fall migrations. Breeding birds such as Acadian flycatcher, hooded warbler, and worm-eating warbler are present, although not commonly seen. From along the scenic access road or the rustic trail, discover abundant wildflowers including the fragile bottle gentian. Rare pickerel frog and a unique species of caddis fly inhabit the gorge. *AVOID DISTURBING ROCKS IN STREAM,* as they support an important invertebrate population. *ACCESS ROAD MAY BE IMPASSABLE IN WINTER.*

*Directions: From Sauk City take US 12 north 8 miles. Turn left (west) on County Hwy. C. Go 1.5 miles to Stone's Pocket Road. Turn right (north), go 2 miles. Several pullouts on left side of road. Trailhead at right bend in road.*

**Ownership:** TNC (608) 251-8140
**Size:** 3,279 acres    **Closest town:** Sauk City

## 53. WILDCAT MOUNTAIN STATE PARK

**Description:** The Kickapoo River flows through this park carving out rugged valleys and bluffs forested with southern hardwoods and hemlocks supporting a diversity of songbirds and mammals.

**Viewing information:** A steep trail climbs Mount Pisgah, past fern and hemlock bluffs, home to wild turkey, ruffed grouse, scarlet tanager, brown creeper, barred owl, pileated and red-headed woodpecker, and white-tailed deer. Breath-taking views atop Pisgah and Wildcat offer sightings of turkey vulture, bald eagle, and migrating broad-winged and rough-legged hawk. Witness the spectacular spring wildflower show. Moles tunnel in fertile river-bottom soils, while American woodcock "peent" on spring evenings. Throughout summer, search river's edge for snipes, belted kingfisher, and Louisiana waterthrush. Summer naturalist programs.

*Directions: From Ontario take WI 33 southeast 2.5 miles.*

**Ownership:** WDNR  (608) 337-4775
**Size:** 3,500 acres    **Closest town:** Ontario

## REGION FIVE: CENTRAL SANDS TRANSITION

Ten thousand years ago, vast glacial Lake Wisconsin formed from the melting of glaciers. The lake drained, leaving a large, flat landscape. Fire maintained uplands of sandy oak savanna and pine barrens, where prairie flowers and grasses flourished. Peat and muck-lined basins filled with sedges, bulrushes, cattails, and cranberries, with willow and tag alder along their rims. Wisconsin's "tension zone," where northern and southern species meet, is especially diverse.

Wetlands here are home to sandhill crane, Canada goose, mallard, and blue-winged teal. Coyotes hunt the lowlands, which support the bittern, black tern, beaver, otter, muskrat, and mink. In the oak forests, white-tailed deer, chipmunk, gray squirrel, raccoon, chickadee, and ruffed grouse make their homes. The federally-listed endangered Karner blue butterfly inhabits the grasslands where wild lupine blooms.

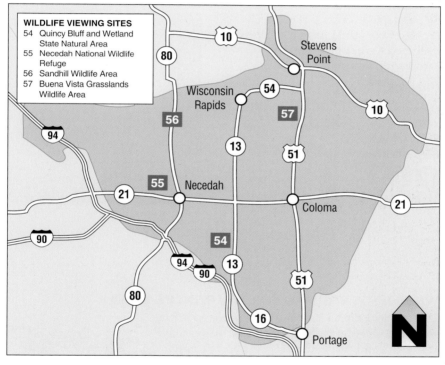

**WILDLIFE VIEWING SITES**
54  Quincy Bluff and Wetland State Natural Area
55  Necedah National Wildlife Refuge
56  Sandhill Wildlife Area
57  Buena Vista Grasslands Wildlife Area

CENTRAL SANDS

67

## 54. QUINCY BLUFF AND WETLAND STATE NATURAL AREA

**Description:** Looming 200 feet above expansive wetlands, the 2-mile long sandstone Quincy Bluff and Lone Rock, a sandstone mesa, harbor northern oak and pine forests among open cliffs. The setting provides stunning vistas reminiscent of pre-European settlement Wisconsin with its unique habitats for rare animals and plants.

**Viewing information:** From paths traversing the property, watch as turkey vultures soar the thermals. Sandhill crane, northern harrier, and marsh birds inhabit the wetlands. Wild turkey and white-tailed deer are attracted to the oak woodland's bounty of acorns. Wild lupine offers prime habitat for the endangered Karner blue butterfly. Good car viewing from adjacent roads.

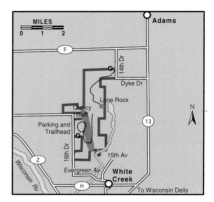

*Directions: See map.*

**Ownership:** TNC (608) 251-8140; WDNR (608) 339-3385
**Size:** 3,338 acres
**Closest town:** White Creek

## WILDLIFE WATCHING FOR THE WINTER-WEARY

Don't underestimate the fun you can have watching wildlife during the bleakest months of the year. Insect galls, and bird, squirrel, and hornet nests once hidden by summer foliage are easily spotted. Snowy winters are best for tracking. Look for deer, fox, rabbit, squirrel, raccoon, opossum, porcupine, and skunk tracks in the snow. Some common bird tracks include wild turkey, raven, and crow. Sometimes the drama can be incredible, as when you follow rabbit tracks that end with a hungry great horned owl's wingprints. Meadow vole tunnels become very pronounced and mink tracks may be found along streams. Get a good field guide to tracks and entertain yourself on those long, cold winter weekends.

# 55. NECEDAH NATIONAL WILDLIFE REFUGE

**Description:** This refuge is part of the Great Central Wisconsin Swamp, which formerly encompassed some 7,800 square miles. The vast expanse of sedge meadow, marsh, and hardwood forest supports an abundance of wildlife.

**Viewing information:** A self-guided auto tour and interpretive foot trail winds through this varied habitat. On flowages, look and listen for common loon, bald eagle, osprey, spring peeper, and wood frog. Herons, bitterns, black tern, yellow-headed blackbird, and marsh wren are common sights spring through fall, as are beaver, muskrat, mink, and otter. In drier sedge meadows, coyotes stalk sandhill cranes. Look for Canada goose, tundra swan, black duck, pintail, blue-winged and green-winged teal, and American wigeon spring and fall. Spring is best for songbird migration when warblers, vireos, orioles, tanagers, and grosbeaks migrate through. Badger, raccoon, and skunk dig up turtle nests on the dikes. Black bear, white-tailed deer, squirrel, ruffed grouse, and wild turkey inhabit the forests. An observation tower provides a panoramic view of the marsh-sedge meadow complex. *REFUGE ROADS MAY BE IMPASSABLE DUE TO FLOODING OR SNOW. CALL AHEAD.*

**Directions:** *From Necedah go 5 miles west on WI 21 to refuge headquarters on right.*

**Ownership:** USFWS  (608) 565-2551
**Size:** 43,636 acres    **Closest town:** Necedah

*The federally-listed endangered Karner blue butterfly is found exclusively among fields of wild lupine wildflowers upon which it feeds. Look for the butterfly and its host plant in sandy areas of the state from Crex Meadows to Sandhill Wildlife Area to Chiwaukee Prairie.*

A.B. SHELDON

# 56. SANDHILL WILDLIFE AREA

**Description:** In the heart of the Central Sands country, Sandhill's big white-tailed bucks, extraordinary abundance of wildlife, and superb viewing opportunities make it one of the state's premier wildlife viewing areas.

**Viewing information:** The 14-mile, self-guided Trumpeter Trail Auto Tour meanders through hardwood forests, sedge meadows, flowages, oak savannas, and dry prairies. In mid-April, witness the incredible courtship dance of the sandhill crane. In March, April, September, and October, flowages fill with migrating Canada goose, teal, mallard, and wood duck. Spring warbler migration peaks in early May. In the grasslands look for eastern bluebird, badger, red-tailed hawk, coyote, and the federally-listed endangered Karner blue butterfly as it flits from one wild lupine bouquet to another. Summer is great for viewing herons, beaver, muskrat, and mink. Watch for white-tailed deer, especially in the rutting season from October through November. Special wildlife management practices encourage older, larger deer. In late October visit Gallagher Marsh before sunrise, and witness the largest concentration of staging sandhills in the state—3,000 to 5,000 cranes congregate each fall. A small herd of bison roams within an enclosed 260-acre prairie restoration area. Observation towers at 3 sites provide good overviews of the landscape. A rustic hiking trail with boardwalks allows closeup access to a variety of habitats. Cross-country skiing allows excellent winter wildlife viewing and tracking. An Outdoor Skills Center offers wildlife watching programs. *PLEASE ADHERE TO POSTED HOURS AT ENTRANCE. AUTO TOUR ROUTE ONLY PASSABLE MID-APRIL THROUGH OCTOBER. CALL AHEAD.*

**Directions:** *From Babcock take WI 80 south. Turn right on County Hwy. X. Go 1 mile to entrance on left side of road.*

**Ownership:** WDNR (715) 884-2437
**Size:** 9,460 acres    **Closest town:** Babcock

Wisconsin wildlife managers and foresters work together to regenerate communities of oak, aspen, and jack pine. These trees must have full sun to sprout from seeds or roots, and this requires the nearly complete removal of the older trees. While clearcutting may at first appear ragged and unnatural, the rapid flourish of lush growth provides excellent food and cover for a diversity of wildlife including chestnut-sided warbler, goshawk, blue-spotted salamander, gray wolf, deer, bear, bobcat, turkey, ruffed grouse, and woodcock.

# 57. BUENA VISTA GRASSLANDS WILDLIFE AREA

**Description:** This vast grassland landscape supports Wisconsin's largest remnant population of greater prairie chickens.

**Viewing information:** Witness the spring pre-dawn territorial breeding display of the threatened greater prairie chicken. *VIEWING ACTIVITIES ARE CLOSELY CONTROLLED AND ALLOWED ONLY FROM BLINDS TO PREVENT DISTURBANCE OF THE BIRDS.* During other seasons of the year, enjoy the abundant eastern and western meadowlark, bobolink, grassland sparrows, upland sandpiper, sandhill crane, northern harrier, and American kestrel. Look for badger and Franklin's ground squirrel. Observe from the public roads on viewing route or walk through the grassland. State property marked with yellow prairie chicken signs. Roadside parking only. Observation blinds are available daily beginning early April (fee/reservations). *RESPECT RIGHTS OF PRIVATE PROPERTY OWNERS.*

**Directions:** *See map.*

**Ownership:** WDNR (608) 339-3385; Blind reservations (715) 346-4109; Dane County Conservation League; Wisconsin Society for Ornithology

**Size:** 12,000 acres
**Closest town:** Bancroft

*Reserving a blind at Buena Vista Grasslands Wildlife Area can provide an unobtrusive place to watch the pre-dawn breeding display of the greater prairie chickens. Males arrive to dance on the "booming grounds" as winter melts into spring.*
GERARD FUEHRER

**CENTRAL SANDS**

# REGION 6: SOUTHEASTERN MORAINES

If glaciers had bones, this region would resemble a graveyard. Medieval names describe the deposits left behind as the continental ice sheets melted away: drumlins, kames, eskers, moraines, kettles. The mile-high ice molded the land into a series of ridges and lowlands, where pure stands of tallgrass prairie were interrupted by oak savanna, southern hardwood forest, and cattail wetlands. Much of this region is now under cultivation or urban development.

Cottontail rabbit, red fox, coyote, crow, and song sparrow are found in "edge" habitats, where field meets forest. Gray squirrel, chipmunk, thrush, and vireo take to the woods, while badger, woodchuck, thirteen-lined ground squirrel, upland sandpiper, and bobolink stake their claims in the grasslands. Marshes teem with mink, muskrat, beaver, red-winged and yellow-headed blackbird, swamp sparrow, marsh wren, and sandhill crane.

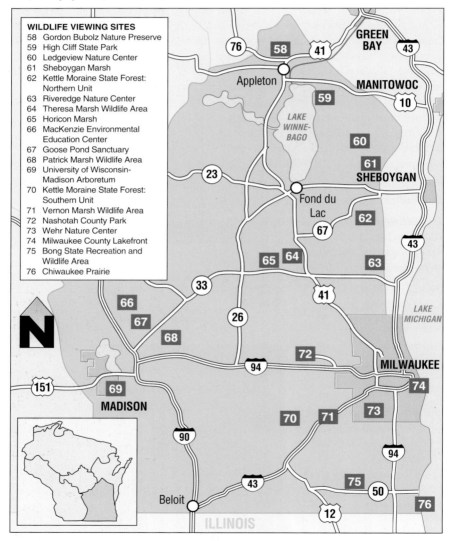

**WILDLIFE VIEWING SITES**
58 Gordon Bubolz Nature Preserve
59 High Cliff State Park
60 Ledgeview Nature Center
61 Sheboygan Marsh
62 Kettle Moraine State Forest: Northern Unit
63 Riveredge Nature Center
64 Theresa Marsh Wildlife Area
65 Horicon Marsh
66 MacKenzie Environmental Education Center
67 Goose Pond Sanctuary
68 Patrick Marsh Wildlife Area
69 University of Wisconsin-Madison Arboretum
70 Kettle Moraine State Forest: Southern Unit
71 Vernon Marsh Wildlife Area
72 Nashotah County Park
73 Wehr Nature Center
74 Milwaukee County Lakefront
75 Bong State Recreation and Wildlife Area
76 Chiwaukee Prairie

## 58. GORDON BUBOLZ NATURE PRESERVE

**Description:** Located at the headwaters of Bear Creek, large stands of white cedar and lowland hardwood forest make this preserve a haven for ferns and mosses, white-tailed deer, and songbirds.

**Viewing information:** Laced with hard-packed trails, the cedar swamp is ideal habitat for deer—the herd peaks at more than 100 in January. Birding is excellent during severe winters; look for pine grosbeak, red crossbill, and red squirrel. As the weather warms, witness a host of migrating warblers, including palm, chestnut-sided, and Nashville. Look for Wilson's and yellow warbler, snipe, and woodcock in the willow and dogwood thickets bordering the meadow. Brush piles on Deer Run Trail harbor cottontail rabbits in winter, thirteen-lined ground squirrels in summer, and mice year-round. Northern harrier nest in the old meadow. From a barrier-free viewing platform, watch brook and rainbow trout in the pond. In summer, look for red-bellied snake, very large fox snake, and painted and mud turtle. Earth-sheltered nature center has programs and exhibits, including a bee observation hive.

***Directions:*** *From Appleton take US 10 west. Take US 41 north. Turn right (east) on County Hwy. OO. Turn left (north) on County Hwy. A. Go 1.7 miles; entrance on left.*

**Ownership:** Natural Areas Preservation, Inc. (PVT) (414) 731-6041
**Size:** 762 acres   **Closest town:** Appleton

*The red squirrel, a common inhabitant of pine woods, is active year-round. Look for "cone cobs" beneath pines where these little squirrels have dined. The "cobs" are the remains of the cones, after the squirrels have removed the nutritious seeds hidden deep within.*

JOHN GERLACH

73

**Description:** On the northeastern shores of Lake Winnebago, High Cliff's hardwood forests and open waters are home to a diversity of wildlife.

**Viewing information:** From bluffs, enjoy a spectacular panoramic view of Wisconsin's largest inland lake. Woodlands come alive each spring with migratory birds including rose-breasted grosbeak, scarlet tanager, and a host of warblers, including Tennessee and northern parula. At dusk, listen to whip-poor-will and nighthawk. Along the shores look for red-shouldered hawk, osprey, herring gull, sandpiper, and cliff swallow. Diving and puddle ducks favor the open waters. White-tailed deer, red fox, raccoon, eastern chipmunk, and thirteen-lined ground squirrel are common. From barrier-free trails, enjoy spring woodland floral display. Seasonal naturalist programs. Park can be crowded in summer.

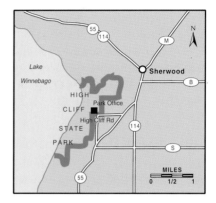

*Directions: See map.*

**Ownership:** WDNR (414) 989-1106
**Size:** 1,145 acres
**Closest town:** Sherwood

## CALLING ALL WILDLIFE

You can become actively involved in enticing wildlife to come to you. By repeating, in a rhythmic manner, the sound "psssh," which imitates scolding birds, or by loudly and repeatedly kissing the back of your hand, which sounds like a scolding squirrel, you can attract chickadees, nuthatches, sparrows, and jays. Or purchase calling devices from a sporting goods store: wild turkey calls, deer bugles or antlers for rattling, owl and crow calls, or predator calls that imitate the squeal of a wounded rabbit. Use calls ethically. Prolonged calling is considered harassing and disruptive. Contact WDNR for regulations.

**Description:** Ledgeview, noted for its cave habitats and resident bats, encompasses forest, prairie, and rocky ledges.

**Viewing information:** Cave spiders, cave crickets, and little brown and big brown bats are the stars here. Common nesters in the hardwood forests include red-eyed vireo, ovenbird, rose-breasted grosbeak, and scarlet tanager. Great crested flycatcher, wood duck, woodpeckers, owls, raccoon, and flying squirrel nest in tree cavities. Look for field sparrow, eastern kingbird, and indigo bunting along wood's edge. DeKay's snake, red fox, and woodchuck inhabit rocky outcrops, while turkey vulture and red-tailed hawk ride the updrafts. Enjoy panoramic views from the observation tower. Interpretive center cave tours offered late spring through fall. Call for reservations.

**Directions:** *From Chilton take County Hwy. G south 1.5 miles. Turn left (east) on Short Road. Entrance on left side.*

**Ownership:** Calumet County (414) 849-7094
**Size:** 105 acres     **Closest town:** Chilton

*Look for the iridescent blue on male indigo buntings as they fly along hedgerows and wooded edges. Listen for the paired phrases of its mating song, even at midday.*
MARK F. WALLNER

SOUTHEASTERN MORAINES

75

## 61. SHEBOYGAN MARSH

**Description:** Wetland wildlife thrive in this marsh complex of lowland hardwoods, sedge meadows, cattail and deep water marsh, all interspersed with cedar-tamarack swamps more characteristic of Wisconsin's Northern Highlands.

**Viewing information:** Best viewing of marshland river wildlife is by canoe. Look for yellow-headed blackbird, green and blue-winged teal, mallard, black duck, wood duck, Canada goose, sora, Virginia rail, and pied-billed grebe. Beaver, muskrat, and river otter leave tracks on shorelines. In spring, hear the chorus of American toads and spring peepers. Sandhill cranes breed in the drier meadows. Red-shouldered hawks make infrequent appearances, while northern harrier and great horned owl are more common. Broad-winged hawks migrate through each spring. From surrounding roads, enjoy good car-viewing of white-tailed deer in fields at dawn and dusk. Maps, canoe and boat rentals at park lodge. *MAP RECOMMENDED. PLEASE RESPECT REFUGE AREA CLOSURE SIGNS.*

*Directions: From Elkhart Lake take County Hwy. J northeast to the Marsh Park Lodge entrance.*

**Ownership:** Sheboygan County (414) 459-3060;
Marsh Park Lodge (414) 876-2535; WDNR (414) 892-8756; PVT
**Size:** 14,000 acres    **Closest town:** Elkhart Lake

*River otters feed on fish, crayfish, insects, and amphibians and can be found near lakes and streams. Look for their tracks along the shoreline and "slips" worn into the mud where otters slide down banks.* MARK S. WERNER

## 62. KETTLE MORAINE STATE FOREST: NORTHERN UNIT

**Description:** The abundance of wildlife here is phenomenal. Rolling glacial topography supports cattail marsh, climax hardwood forests, lakes, alder thickets, prairies, cedar/tamarack swamps, and black spruce bogs.

**Viewing information:** Kettle Moraine Scenic Drive winds through the heart of this outstanding unit of the Ice Age National Scientific Reserve. Kettle Moraine Lake is noteworthy for spring migration of merganser, scaup, bufflehead, canvasback, and ruddy duck. Spruce Lake Bog State Natural Area contains black spruce, a tree typical of northern bogs. A boardwalk traverses this fragile area. *PLEASE STAY ON BOARDWALK: GROUND SURFACE IS UNSTABLE, CONTAINS POISON SUMAC.* Birds here are typical of northern Wisconsin: alder flycatcher, black-and-white warbler, and northern waterthrush. At Jersey Flats, visit the prairie restoration project where bobolink, dickcissel, eastern meadowlark, and northern harrier nest. Forested trail around Mauthe Lake offers good birding. From barrier-free viewing platform, watch for the threatened long-eared sunfish. Haskell Noyes Memorial Forest State Natural Area contains a remnant climax forest that shelters Acadian flycatcher, cerulean warbler, and yellow-throated vireo. A hike up the trail may yield red-shouldered hawk, hooded warbler, pileated woodpecker, wild turkey, barred owl, great crested flycatcher, red-eyed vireo, scarlet tanager, and rose-breasted grosbeak. In the second week of October, watch for the woodcock and snipe migration. Resident mammals include white-tailed deer, beaver, muskrat, mink, badger, coyote, woodchuck, cottontail rabbit, and raccoon. Stop at Ice Age Visitor Center for maps, exhibits, seasonal naturalist programs, and information on the Ice Age Trail.

***Directions:*** *From Campbellsport take WI 67 northeast 7 miles. Follow signs to Ice Age Interpretive Center which is south on County Hwy. G.*

**Ownership:** WDNR (414) 533-8322
**Size:** 27,768 acres    **Closest town:** Campbellsport

Wisconsin provides rest stops and nesting areas for a wide array of thrushes, warblers, vireos, flycatchers, and many species of waterfowl. These birds, called "neotropical migrants," spend the summer in the U.S. or Canada and fly to Central and South America for the fall to carry out their lives in warmer climates. Due to alterations in breeding, resting, and wintering habitats, these neotropical birds are declining dramatically in number. Programs such as "Partners in Flight" and the "North American Waterfowl Management Plan" are working to find ways to bridge the gap between habitats.

# 63. RIVEREDGE NATURE CENTER

**Description:** Adjacent to the Milwaukee River and encompassing Riveredge Creek, this site contains a variety of wetlands, upland forests, and restored prairies that attract numerous songbirds and amphibians.

**Viewing information:** Trails and boardwalks wander through a diversity of habitats. Viewing platforms overlook shallow seasonal ponds where blue-spotted salamander, chorus and eastern gray treefrog, spring peeper, American toad, and fairy shrimp abound. Bullfrogs breed in the river as do suckers, a bottom-feeding migratory fish. Songbird migration peaks in mid-May when the blue-winged warbler, scarlet tanager, rose-breasted grosbeak, yellow-throated vireo, and blue-gray gnatcatcher begin breeding. Red-shouldered and Cooper's hawk nest here, while rough-legged hawk and saw-whet owl migrate through. Common mammals include muskrat, chipmunk, woodchuck, coyote, red and gray fox, raccoon, and white-tailed deer. Dramatic displays of trillium and spring beauty. Interpretive center offers exhibits, maps, seasonal programs.

**Directions:** *In Newburg take WI 33 east. Turn left on County Hwy. Y (Hawthorne Drive). Go northeast about 1 mile. Entrance is on right.*

**Ownership:** Riveredge Nature Center, Inc. (414) 675-6888
**Size:** 350 acres    **Closest town:** Newburg

A little frog with a big voice, the spring peeper fills the early spring air with a song that can be heard for a quarter of a mile or more. In chorus, the peeps of hundreds of frogs combine to form a sound reminiscent of sleighbells. Listen and look for these amphibians near ponds and other wetlands in early April.

A.B. SHELDON

## 64. THERESA MARSH WILDLIFE AREA

**Description:** Noted for its excellent waterfowl viewing, this wetland complex provides feeding and resting areas for thousands of geese and ducks.

**Viewing information:** Enjoy excellent early morning and dusk car-viewing of migrating Canada geese from WI 28 pullout. Also watch for wood duck, blue-winged teal, pintail, sandpipers, rails, herons, common egret, sandhill crane, and belted kingfisher. Peak waterfowl migration is from mid-September through early December and again mid-March through April. Rough-legged hawks may be found in winter. Hear spring peeper and chorus frog in spring, as warblers and vireos pass through. Muskrat, red fox, raccoon, and white-tailed deer thrive here. Except during fall, most of marsh is open to foot travel on dikes. *USE CAUTION ON WI 28 PULLOUT.*

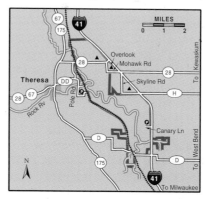

**Directions:** *See map.*

**Ownership:** WDNR (414) 644-5248; PVT
**Size:** 5,500 acres
**Closest town:** Theresa

## IN PASSIVE PURSUIT OF WILDLIFE

When you walk into a wildlife viewing area, the featured birds and mammals often take flight or run in the opposite direction of your approach. Find a warm, dry, comfortable place to sit, lean back against a rock or tree, and relax. Remember to remain perfectly still while you wait. This is a tough technique for the impatient and wiggly, but if performed well, you will be rewarded with memorable sights.

## 65. HORICON MARSH

**Description:** Horicon Marsh is designated as a Wetland of International Importance. The largest freshwater cattail marsh in the country, it is the most popular wildlife viewing area in Wisconsin. Observe hundreds of thousands of geese and ducks during migration.

**Viewing information:** Spring and fall are excellent seasons to view migrating Canada geese whose numbers peak at about 250,000 late October to mid-November. More than 20 species of ducks, including green-winged teal, American wigeon, northern shoveler, scaup, gadwall, and pintail also migrate through. Blue-winged teal, redhead, mallard, ruddy duck, coot, black tern, and yellow-headed blackbird nest on the marsh. Fourmile Island State Natural Area supports the largest heron and egret nesting colony in Wisconsin. *VIEW FROM BOAT ONLY. NO ENTRY ONTO FOURMILE ISLAND ALLOWED.* The marsh's more unique and secretive inhabitants such as the moorhen, sora, Virginia rail, pied-billed grebe, and American bittern are best viewed along the state canoe trail. Muskrat, mink, and otter cavort in the water, while white-tailed deer, red fox, raccoon, skunk, opossum, and coyote inhabit the woods and grasslands. During warm months, swallows, sandhill crane, and monarch butterfly share these uplands. Boat rentals and tours available in Horicon. *STOPPING ALONG WI 49 IS DANGEROUS, PLEASE USE PARKING LOTS.* **Information on federal, state, and private areas of Horicon Marsh follows.**

**USFWS National Wildlife Refuge:** For protection of habitat and wildlife, access limited to specified areas only: WI 49 scenic overlook with exhibit; Federal Dike Road; 3 hiking trails with barrier-free boardwalk; seasonal auto tour route. *CANOEING NOT PERMITTED. OTHER IMPORTANT RESTRICTIONS APPLY.* Contact Refuge Headquarters for maps and information.

**WDNR State Wildlife Area:** Hiking and canoe trails. Education center has maps and seasonal interpretive programs.

**Marsh Haven Nature Center (pvt):** Maps, information, and programs, April to November. Observation tower, trails, entry fee.

***Directions:*** *See map opposite page.*

**Ownership:** USFWS (414) 387-2658; WDNR (414) 387-7860; Marsh Haven Nature Center (414) 324-5818

**Size:** 32,000 acres     **Closest Towns:** Horicon for State Headquarters, Waupun for Federal Refuge and Nature Center

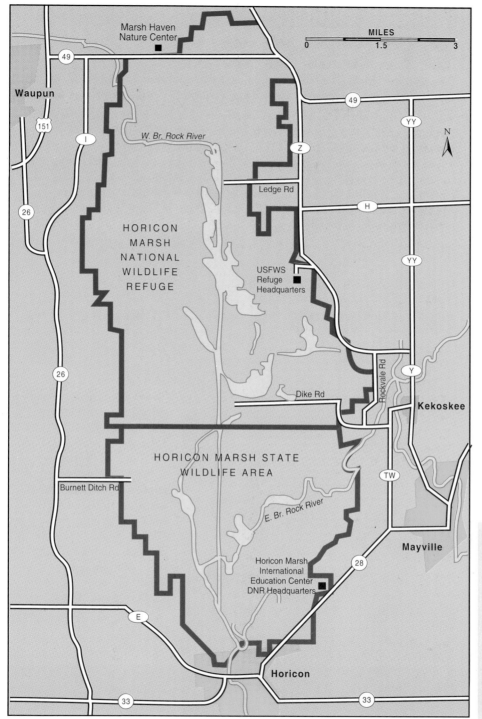

Marsh Haven
Nature Center

MILES
0        1.5        3

Waupun

49

151

26

W. Br. Rock River

I

Z

Ledge Rd

H

49

YY

N

YY

HORICON
MARSH
NATIONAL
WILDLIFE
REFUGE

USFWS
Refuge
Headquarters

26

Rockvale Rd

Y

Dike Rd

Kekoskee

HORICON MARSH STATE
WILDLIFE AREA

Burnett Ditch Rd

TW

E. Br. Rock River

Mayville

28

Horicon Marsh
International
Education Center
DNR Headquarters

E

Horicon

33                    33

# 66. MACKENZIE ENVIRONMENTAL EDUCATION CENTER

**Description:** This residential education center encompasses rolling fields and forests, restored tallgrass prairie, a native live animal exhibit, and free-roaming wildlife.

**Viewing information:** April and May provide excellent birding with a wide diversity of warblers and vireos attracted to the forest. The butterfly garden lures monarchs in summer. Some of Wisconsin's more elusive native wildlife are found at the live animal exhibit: gray wolf, fox, fisher, badger, porcupine, bobcat, and lynx as well as white-tailed deer, bison, eagle, hawks, and owls. The barrier-free Wildlife Trail demonstrates a variety of wildlife management practices. Stop at the "Aliens Museum" for exhibits of non-native wildlife. Grounds and exhibit hours vary. Check with center.

**Directions:** *Take US 51 north to Poynette. Turn right on County Hwy. CS. Go about 1 mile to entrance on right.*

**Ownership:** WDNR  (608) 635-4498
**Size:** 280 acres    **Closest town:** Poynette

Listen for the "hoot...hoot...hoot" of the great horned owl at dusk and dawn, prominent December through February. In the twilight, watch for a hawk-like silhouette with round head and short neck coasting low from forest to field. During the day, listen for the caws of crows which often taunt these tree-roosting raptors.

GERARD FUEHRER

## 67. GOOSE POND SANCTUARY

**Description:** A prairie pothole in the former Empire Prairie, Goose Pond attracts a rich variety of wetland and grassland birds.

**Viewing information:** Best viewing is from late March through late November. Presence of unusual shorebirds, such as black-bellied and lesser golden plover, dunlin, Hudsonian godwit, and dowitcher, varies with water level. During spring and fall migration, large concentrations of Canada and snow goose, tundra swan, and ducks flock in. Federally-listed endangered peregrine falcons make occasional stops. Ruddy duck, yellow-headed blackbird, and marsh wren nest around the pond, while common egret and great blue heron make regular late summer visits. American kestrel, northern harrier, muskrat, tiger salamander, chorus and treefrog, and Blanding's turtle also spend warm months here. A self-guided trail winds through a portion of the state's largest tallgrass prairie restoration allowing a close glimpse of bobolink, dickcissel, and sedge wren. Pullout, permanently mounted spotting scope, and an information board are on dead-end Prairie Lane off Goose Pond road. Group tours. *PLEASE STAY ON ROADS OR TRAIL.*

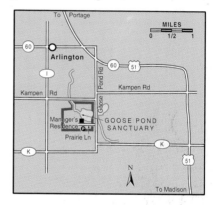

**Directions:** *See map.*

**Ownership:** Madison Audubon Society (608) 635-4160 or (608) 255-BIRD.
**Size:** 174 acres
**Closest town:** Arlington

East central Wisconsin is the site of a unique habitat restoration project in the midst of a large rural landscape. The Glacial Habitat Restoration Area spans portions of Winnebago, Fond Du Lac, Dodge, and Columbia counties. Here, wildlife managers are working with private landowners to restore grasslands and wetlands, thus demonstrating how wildlife and agriculture can coexist.

SOUTHEASTERN MORAINES

Bobolink

Yellow-faced Bee

Indian Grass

Purple
Coneflower

Prairie
Coneflower

Karner Blue Butterfly

Prairie Chicken

Lupine

13-lined Ground Squirrel

American
Kestrel

Big
Bluestem

Eastern
Meadowla

Prairie Do

Sandhill Crane

Compass Plant

Upland Plove

Indigo

Badger

Prairie Ringneck Snake

Sideoats

Little Bluestem

Meadow Vole

## PRAIRIES: LIFE BY FIRE

Historically, wildfires played a very important role in shaping prairies. Fire pushes back the forest and allows the soil to warm up quickly promoting rapid regrowth. Prairies once covered two million acres of Wisconsin. As Europeans arrived, they converted the treeless, fertile prairies into crop fields and controlled the sweep of wildfires. Today, less than 12,000 scattered acres exist. As grasslands are lost, so are the associated animals. In order to protect and maintain the biodiversity of prairie ecosystems, special restoration techniques, such as prescribed or controlled burning, can give grasslands a chance for rebirth.

## 68. PATRICK MARSH WILDLIFE AREA

**Description:** The largest colony of yellow-headed blackbirds in southern Wisconsin once resided in the shallow waters of Patrick Lake. But in the early 1960s, this site was drained and continuously farmed until 1992, when the wetland was restored through cooperative efforts of WDOT and WDNR. Patrick Lake has since made a quick and remarkable transformation, rebounding into an enticing shallow marsh for waterfowl.

**Viewing information:** Virtually all of Wisconsin's migratory waterfowl, from blue-winged teal, ruddy duck, and hooded merganser to Canada goose and tundra swan can be found here in great numbers spring and fall. Exposed mudflats lure shorebirds, including spotted sandpiper, dunlin, and semi-palmated plover. Numerous waterfowl species nest here throughout summer. Good viewing along Stone Quarry Road.

*Directions: In Sun Prairie take US 151 northeast to exit 103 (N. Bristol Road). Go north then turn right on Wilburn; go 0.5 mile. Turn right on Columbus St. Go under US 151. Turn left on Stone Quarry Road. Site is on right with limited off-road parking.*

**Ownership:** WDNR (608) 275-3242
**Size:** 270 acres    **Closest town:** Sun Prairie


## IN ACTIVE PURSUIT OF WILDLIFE: TRACKING AND STALKING

Tracking wildlife involves searching for tracks in snow, mud, and sand, or following well-worn trails made by routine passages of animals such as deer, rabbits, or meadow voles. Though you may never spot the animal, you can tell a great deal about it, its habits and preferred habitat. Stalking wildlife usually occurs after you've spotted an animal in the distance. This technique requires the use of all your senses in order to get close without its noticing you Keep the wind in your face, walk quietly, avoid brittle leaves or sticks, and keep vegetation between you and it.

## 69. UNIVERSITY OF WISCONSIN-MADISON ARBORETUM

**Description:** URBAN SITE. A unique haven in a bustling urban center, this site is a microcosm of pre-European settlement Wisconsin, and world-renowned for its collection of restored native plant and animal communities.

**Viewing information:** In spring, wildflowers emerge as chorus frogs serenade in wet woodlands. May is excellent for viewing an incredible variety of migratory birds, including yellow-rumped warbler and red-eyed vireo. In summer, meander through Curtis Prairie, the world's first tallgrass prairie restoration, where hosts of butterflies flutter over a parade of prairie flowers. Annual cicadas and crickets drone as goldfinches gather thistle seed. In the cool boreal forest, chickadees flit overhead. The pond is filled with mallard, teal, and an occasional mink. In September, woodchuck, gray squirrel, and chipmunk prepare for winter. Look for an occasional fox and weasel. More than 20 miles of trails and firelanes. McKay Visitor Center offers information, tours, and programs.

**Directions:** *In Madison take US 12/18 to Seminole Highway exit. Travel north a short distance to arboretum entrance on right side of Seminole Highway.*

**Ownership:** University of Wisconsin-Madison (608) 263-7888
**Size:** 1,280 acres    **Closest town:** Madison

*Digging is a way of life for the badger, the official state animal. The dens of these elusive mammals, built into hillsides or grassy areas with a fan-shaped mound of dirt at the entrance, are much easier to spot than the animal itself.* MARK S. WERNER

SOUTHEASTERN MORAINES

87

# 70. KETTLE MORAINE STATE FOREST: SOUTHERN UNIT

**Description:** A vestige of glaciers that scoured Wisconsin more than 10,000 years ago, this site's moraines, eskers, kettle ponds and lakes, and sand plains are cloaked with oak forests, dry and wet prairies, and wetlands with an abundance of wildlife.

**Viewing information:** The Lapham Peak unit, on County Hwy. C just north of US 18, contains an observation tower that offers a panoramic vista of glaciated country. Wild turkey and deer are found along wooded and meadow trails. In the Southern Unit, travel through hills of oak and pine along Scuppernong Trail in quest of rufous-sided towhee, blue-gray gnatcatcher, and pileated woodpecker. Sand prairie, bottomland forest, marsh, creek, and pond on Scuppernong Springs Nature Trail shelter warblers, barred owl, Canada goose, and wood duck. Amidst the complex of prairie, marsh, and sedge meadow in Scuppernong Marsh along the Ice Age Trail, find eastern bluebird, western meadowlark, short-eared owl, and sandhill crane. Large, shallow LaGrange Lake is great for watching common merganser and pied-billed grebe. Discover thirteen-lined ground squirrel in the grassy areas near Ottawa Lake, which can be explored from a self-guided canoe trail. Look for great blue heron, black tern, and muskrat. Paradise Springs offers a paved hand-cord trail for visually-impaired visitors. Clear waters afford glimpses of brook and rainbow trout from a barrier-free viewing platform. Survey roadside fields for white-tailed deer at dawn and dusk. Visitor center has maps, information, exhibits, and programs.

*Directions:* *From Eagle travel 3 miles west on WI 59 to headquarters on left.*

**Ownership:** WDNR (414) 594-2135
**Size:** 20,000 acres     **Closest town:** Eagle

Humans have so disrupted the natural environment that it is now necessary to actively manage habitats to provide the food, water, and shelter that many wildlife need to survive. An important point to remember is that whenever any habitat is modified, whether by urban development, plowing, prescribed burning, clearcutting, mowing, grazing, or by letting natural succession proceed at its slow interminable pace, some wildlife will find the changes unsuitable, while others will respond favorably.

# 71. VERNON MARSH WILDLIFE AREA

**Description:** Though over 90 percent of southeastern Wisconsin wetlands have been lost, Vernon Marsh, with its actively managed flowages and grasslands, remains to provide a haven for migrating waterfowl and songbirds.

**Viewing information:** Spring is the best viewing season. Walk the dikes or paddle a canoe through the impoundments to the Fox River. Look for yellow-headed blackbird, common and black tern, sandhill crane, common egret, and great blue heron. Blue-winged teal, giant Canada goose, and wood duck nest in the marsh, while bufflehead, canvasback, green-winged teal, northern shoveler, and wigeon pause briefly in the flooded marshes. Come summer, frogs leap from underfoot as Blanding's and painted turtles bask in the sun and common yellowthroat and marsh wren nest in cattails. Dickcissel and bobolink fill the grasslands. Northern harriers cruise low in search of small mammals, while red-tailed hawks circle above for rabbits, snakes, and Franklin's ground squirrels. Deer venture down to water's edge at dusk while raccoons cast about for crustaceans and fish. Spring wildflower display. Two refuges are closed between September 1-November 30.

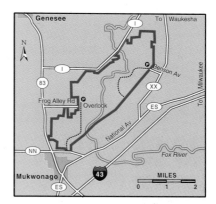

**Directions:** *See map.*

**Ownership:** WDNR (414) 594-2135
**Size:** 3,755 acres
**Closest town:** Mukwonago

*Canada geese are familiar residents of Wisconsin's wetlands from spring to fall. Migrating flocks nest as far north as Hudson Bay and winter in southern Illinois: A subspecies, the giant Canada goose, may be found year-round, especially in urban areas.*

DENVER BRYAN

## 72. NASHOTAH COUNTY PARK

**Description:** Oak woodlands and savanna cloak glacial hills that rise from marshes, cedar glades, and two shallow lakes. These communities attract songbirds and waterfowl.

**Viewing information:** Trails wind through rolling terrain of a pre-settlement landscape. Early spring brings scaup, northern shoveler, blue-winged teal, and wood duck. May brings waves of passing warblers. Rose-breasted grosbeak, eastern wood-pewee, and great crested flycatcher all nest here. Great blue and green heron stalk the shallow waters. Cooper's hawk, and great horned and barred owl search the woodlands for rabbits, mice, and songbirds. Red and gray fox, white-tailed deer, and woodchuck are common.

**Directions:** *From Hartland go 3 miles west on US 16. Turn right on County Hwy. C. Go 0.5 mile to park entrance on left.*

**Ownership:** Waukesha County (414) 548-7790
**Size:** 450 acres　**Closest town:** Hartland

## 73. WEHR NATURE CENTER

**Description:** URBAN SITE. This nature reserve embraces hardwood forest, lake, sedge meadow, marsh, oak savanna, and prairie, and remains a refuge for wildlife away from human development.

**Viewing information:** April and May bring migrants like yellow-rumped, black-and-white, and Wilson's warbler. Gray catbird and indigo bunting seek shelter near the nature center. Red fox, great horned owl, and sharp-shinned and Cooper's hawk are local predators. Mourning cloak and monarch butterfly enjoy the prairie and moist woodlands. Canada geese reside on the small lake where muskrat mounds dot the water. Look for chickadee and woodpecker at the center's feeder in winter. Self-guided nature trail has viewing blind. Center offers exhibits and programs.

**Directions:** *In Hales Corners travel south on WI 100. Turn left (east) onto College Avenue. Nature Center located on south side of College Avenue between WI 100 and South 92nd Street.*

**Ownership:** Milwaukee County Parks (414) 425-8550
**Size:** 220 acres　**Closest town:** Hales Corners

**Description:** URBAN SITE. Milwaukee's unique network of parks and greenways supports a surprising array of wildlife. The Lake Michigan shoreline, on an important migration corridor, attracts songbirds to its forested ravines, and waterfowl, gulls, and terns to its protected bays.

**Viewing information:** Doctor's and Lake parks to the north and Grant Park to the south offer bluff-top vistas of Lake Michigan. Pathways traverse deep hardwood ravines revealing cedar waxwing, finches, and waves of warblers in spring and fall. Other residents include eastern chipmunk, gray squirrel, raccoon, opossum, cottontail rabbit, woodchuck, and occasional red fox and white-tailed deer. Juneau Park Lagoon supports a variety of waterfowl. From park walkways and the municipal pier to the south, scan the harbor for common goldeneye, bufflehead, oldsquaw, and red-breasted merganser from late October through mid-April. Caspian, black, and common tern are frequent migrants. A current city map will show detailed access to these areas. *STOPPING ALONG MEMORIAL DRIVE CAN BE DANGEROUS.* Parks can be crowded in summer.

**Directions:** *See map.*

**Ownership:** Milwaukee County Parks (414) 257-5100

**Size:** NA　**Closest town:** Milwaukee

*The trees along the Milwaukee County Lakefront provide excellent nesting cover for this cedar waxwing and its chicks in spring.* JOHN GERLACH

**SOUTHEASTERN MORAINES**

**Description:** This property's flat expanses are an artifact of a scuttled Air Force Base. The wildlife management program has restored native communities to this altered landscape and wildlife has responded well.

**Viewing information:** Grassland birds and beaver are the key attraction. Prime birding occurs in spring. American robin and red-winged blackbird arrive in early March followed by yellow-headed blackbird. March and April bring a parade of migrating wood duck, shoveler, pintail, and gadwall. Restored prairie grasses and flowers provide habitat for bobolink, upland sandpiper, eastern meadowlark, and sandhill crane. Each May, woodlands fill with a host of spring warblers such as chestnut-sided, bay-breasted, Blackburnian, and Wilson's. Autumn and winter bring occasional osprey, bald eagle, short-eared owl, and snow bunting. White-tailed deer, coyote, red and gray fox, raccoon, woodchuck, chipmunk, thirteen-lined ground squirrel, muskrat, and mink are resident mammals. At dusk, watch the wetlands for beaver—their felled trees and log lodges are conspicuous. Among several barrier-free viewing structures is a beach ramp leading to East Lake. Exhibits, maps, and programs available at visitor center.

***Directions:*** *From Kenosha take I-94 to WI 142 and travel west 9 miles to entrance on left.*

**Ownership:** WDNR  (414) 878-5600 or 652-0377
**Size:** 4,500 acres    **Closest town:** Kansasville

A number of exotic plants and animals, introduced to Wisconsin from other parts of the world, have posed problems to both native wildlife and habitats. Starlings, house sparrows, mute swans, gypsy moths, zebra mussels, purple loosestrife, and tatarian honeysuckle are just a few of the more problematic types. Find out more about the exotics in your area and how you can help control these pests.

*Chiwaukee Prairie is a rich remnant of tallgrass prairie, hosting more than 400 species of native plants, like these shooting stars. Watch the parade of wildflowers as they change the face of the prairie from early spring through late fall. The prairie is an extremely fragile environment, please stay on trails.*

FRANK OBERLE

**Description:** URBAN SITE. Nestled near Lake Michigan's shore, this small but significant site is a remnant of lowland tallgrass prairie once common in southeastern Wisconsin. One of the richest preserves in the nation for diversity of rare plants, it is home to more than 400 native species.

**Viewing information:** Wildflower viewing is excellent spring through fall, but is especially spectacular in mid-summer when the prairie is in full bloom. Spring and fall bring migrations of broad-winged and sharp-shinned hawk along the lakeshore. Resident herring and ring-billed gull and grassland songbirds such as bobolink, meadowlark, and upland sandpiper are common. Eastern hognose and fox snake may be seen on hot summer days. *IT IS ILLEGAL TO PICK FLOWERS OR COLLECT SEED. PLEASE STAY ON FOOTPATHS TO PROTECT FRAGILE VEGETATION.*

**Directions:** *From I-94 west of Kenosha, take WI 165 two miles east to WI 32. Turn right (south) and travel about 1 mile to 116th Street. Turn left onto 116th Street, cross railroad tracks and turn right onto Marina Road. Turn right onto 121st Street. Go 1 block and turn right onto Al Krampert Trail. Drive a few blocks to the parking lot at Gen Crema Trail (footpath) on your left.*

**Ownership:** TNC (608) 251-5605; WDNR (414) 878-5605
**Size:** 300 acres
**Closest town:** Kenosha

**Once extirpated from the eastern United States due to pesticide contamination, loss of habitat, and human disturbance, the peregrine falcon is making a comeback, though it is still a federally-listed endangered species. In the mid-1970s, captive-reared peregrines were reintroduced into Wisconsin. Today, these birds and their offspring are returning to nest sites at the state capitol, University of Wisconsin-Madison, FirstStar Center in Milwaukee, and Wisconsin Electric Power Company in Kenosha.**

# WILDLIFE INDEX

The index below identifies some of the more interesting, uncommon, or attractive wildlife found in Wisconsin, and some of the best sites for viewing selected species. Many of the animals listed may be viewed at other sites as well. The numbers following each species are site numbers, not page numbers.

## Mammals

badger 3, 9, 10, 19, 38, 40, 46, 56, 57, 66, 62
bat 14, 29, 42, 60
bear, black 2, 3, 5, 7, 9, 11, 14, 16, 18, 19, 32, 42, 55
beaver 2, 7, 8, 10, 14, 15, 17, 18, 19, 32, 44, 46, 49, 56, 61, 75
bison 56, 66
bobcat 2, 7, 18, 19, 25, 66
chipmunk, eastern 24, 42, 59, 63, 69, 74, 75
coyote 3, 5, 7, 8, 14, 21, 24, 32, 42, 49, 50, 55, 63
deer, white-tailed 7, 8, 9, 11, 14, 16, 17, 18, 31, 49, 56, 58, 62, 70
fisher 11, 14, 19, 23
fox, gray 49, 63, 72, 75; red 7, 8, 14, 24, 30, 34, 37, 39, 45, 59, 60, 63, 64, 72
gopher, pocket 3, 18, 19, 40
marten, pine 11, 14, 23
mink 7, 8, 10, 14, 15, 17, 18, 19, 34, 43, 46, 55, 56, 65
muskrat 2, 7, 10, 14, 15, 17, 18, 24, 43, 44, 46, 55, 56, 65
opossum 42, 64, 65, 74
otter 2, 7, 8, 10, 14, 17, 19, 38, 46, 49, 55, 61, 65
porcupine 19, 23, 24, 32, 34
rabbits, cottontail 58, 62, 72, 74; snowshoe hare 2, 7, 18, 19, 23, 25, 32, 33, 34; white-tailed jackrabbit 40
raccoon 8, 10, 17, 34, 62, 64, 74
skunk 38, 55, 65
squirrels, (gray or fox) 16, 18, 44, 69, 74; flying 60; Franklin's ground 18, 57, 71; red 11, 23, 24, 33, 34, 39, 42, 58; thirteen-lined ground 45, 49, 58, 70, 75
wolf, gray 3, 7, 9, 14, 19, 30
woodchuck 3, 45, 49, 60, 63, 69, 72, 74

## Birds

bald eagle 1, 2, 6, 7, 8, 10, 11, 13, 14, 15, 17, 18, 19, 20, 25, 39, 44, 46, 47, 48, 50, 51
blackbird, yellow-headed 61, 65, 68, 71, 75
bluebirds 20, 39, 44, 49, 56
chickadee, black-capped 69, 73
cormorant, double-crested 13, 21, 25, 31, 32, 44
crane, sandhill 18, 22, 25, 37, 38, 54, 56, 57, 61, 70, 71
crossbills 1, 42
ducks 5, 7, 8, 13, 15, 16, 17, 18, 19, 21, 23, 25, 29, 38, 45, 46; diving 4, 10, 34, 39, 59, 62, 65, 68, 71, 72, 74; puddle 4, 10, 47, 50, 55, 56, 59, 61, 65, 68, 71, 72
egrets 45, 47, 50, 64, 71
falcon, peregrine 6, 25, 39, 45, 50, 67
goose, Canada 7, 13, 18, 22, 25, 29, 30, 45, 47, 61, 64, 65; snow 18, 21, 25, 67
grassland birds 3, 9, 14, 16, 20, 44, 45, 57, 75, 76
grosbeaks 1, 14, 31, 58, 59, 60, 62, 63, 72
grouse, ruffed 16, 18, 19, 37, 40, 42, 49, 50, 55; sharp-tailed 9, 18, 19
gulls 1, 4, 5, 31, 33, 34, 38, 59, 74, 76
hawks 1, 3, 5, 6, 11, 14, 18, 19, 20, 33, 37, 38, 42, 44, 47, 60, 61, 63
herons 10, 11, 13, 14, 17, 19, 21, 24, 27, 41, 50, 55, 56, 64, 65, 72
kingfisher 10, 11, 17, 19, 21, 24, 64
loon, common 1, 5, 10, 11, 13, 14, 15, 18, 21, 50, 55
osprey 8, 10, 13, 14, 15, 17, 18, 19, 25, 44, 50
ovenbird 2, 16, 20, 23, 60
owls 1, 2, 14, 18, 29, 31, 34, 42, 46, 49, 61, 70
prairie-chicken, greater 25, 57
raven 2, 14, 33
rookeries 23, 25, 46, 65
shorebirds 1, 2, 4, 5, 6, 25, 29, 31, 67, 68
swan, trumpeter 18, 19, 25; tundra 21, 25, 27, 29, 43, 44, 46, 67, 68
tanager, scarlet 14, 16, 59, 60, 63
thrush 2, 6, 16, 20, 33, 38, 45, 60
turkey, wild 42, 47, 48, 49, 50, 54, 55, 62, 70
vireos 2, 16, 46, 48, 55, 62, 63, 66, 69
vulture, turkey 20, 24, 42, 49, 54, 60
warblers 1, 2, 5, 6, 9, 14, 16, 17, 18, 33, 38, 50, 52, 58, 59, 63, 66, 69, 75
woodcock 58, 62
woodpeckers 2, 34, 40, 44, 47; pileated 5, 14, 25, 31, 46, 47, 49, 50, 53, 62, 70; red-headed 47, 50, 53

## Fish

fish 2, 10, 11, 14, 26, 32, 35, 42, 62

## Invertebrates

butterflies & other invertebrates 5, 14, 19, 38, 46, 48, 54, 56, 60, 69

## Reptiles and Amphibians

frogs & toads 6, 8, 17, 18, 25, 29, 37, 45, 55, 61, 63, 64, 67
salamanders 14, 16, 18, 20, 40, 42, 63, 67
skink 18, 20, 42
snakes 6, 18, 20, 40, 47, 58, 60, 76
turtles 2, 5, 14, 37, 39, 40, 44, 50, 58, 71; Blanding's 18, 20, 39, 42, 67, 71

## Wildflowers

wildflowers 3, 6, 9, 14, 25, 33, 37, 52, 59, 63, 69, 76

# WHERE THE WILD THINGS ARE

Falcon Press puts wildlife viewing secrets at your fingertips with our high-quality, full color guidebooks—the Watchable Wildlife Series. This is the only official series of guides for the National Watchable Wildlife Program: areas featured in the books correspond to official sites across America. And you'll find more than just wildlife. Many sites boast beautiful scenery, interpretive displays, opportunities for hiking, picnics, biking, plus—a little peace and quiet. So pick up one of our Wildlife Viewing Guides today and get close to Mother Nature!

## WATCH THIS PARTNERSHIP WORK

The National Watchable Wildlife Program was formed with one goal in mind: get people actively involved in wildlife appreciation and conservation. Defenders of Wildlife has led the way by coordinating this unique multi-agency program and developing a national network of prime wildlife viewing areas.

Part of the proceeds go to conserve wildlife and wildlife habitat.

Visit your local bookstore for more information or call toll-free for a free catalog of nature-related books and gift ideas.

**1-800-582-2665**
Falcon Press
P.O. Box 1718
Helena, MT 59624